HOW TO BE THE FATHER YOUR CHILDREN **NEED**

CRAIG WILKINSON
BESTSELLING AUTHOR AND DAD COACH

Copyright © 2013
By
Craig Wilkinson
All rights reserved
ISBN: 9781976989735

This book is dedicated to:

The Father of all fathers by whose grace I live

*Luke and Blythe, the two precious lives
I have the privilege of fathering*

*Martinique, my lovely wife whose support
has made this possible*

David and Loraine, my praying parents

CONTENTS

Introduction: The Journey Begins   7

Part One: Fatherhood and Manhood

Chapter 1: Fatherhood Matters	15
Chapter 2: Masculinity Under Fire	25
Chapter 3: Manning Up	39

Part Two: Fatherhood in Action

Chapter 4: Call Out	51
Chapter 5: Validate	65
Chapter 6: Create a Sanctuary	77
Chapter 7: Equip for Life	89

Part Three: The Challenge

Chapter 8: Man in the Mirror	107
Chapter 9: The Man Challenge	121
Chapter 10: The Dad Challenge	145
Chapter 11: The Pledge	165
Chapter 12: The Journey Continues	171

About the Author   176

The Journey Begins

"The heart of a father is the masterpiece of nature."
Abbé Prévost.

This book is the product of a deep personal relationship with the magnificent beauty and awful destructiveness of fatherhood in its many manifestations. I am privileged to be the father of two remarkable children: a son, Luke (19 at the time of writing) and a daughter, Blythe, 16. As a divorced man, my journey as father of these wonderful human beings has been the most challenging and enriching experience of my life.

Much of what I share in this book is drawn from the deep well of this experience. My inner struggle with my own childhood wounds has added another dimension to my understanding of fatherhood and finally my work with men and fatherless children in impoverished communities has contributed to the insights reflected in these pages.

As I write there is an emerging global awareness of the importance of fatherhood. In my own country, South Africa, there is a groundswell of anger at the insanely high levels of rape and abuse of women. More and more research is confirming that fatherlessness is possibly the single biggest driver of social dysfunction in communities around the world. After working in the field of socio-economic development for almost a decade, I concur. Men are in crisis and something serious needs to be done.

Against this bleak backdrop, on my last birthday I received one of the greatest gifts a father could ever hope for. My son Luke wrote me an unsolicited, unexpected letter of thanks and appreciation for the role I have played as his father. I have, with his permission, reproduced the unedited letter here, as it portrays sentiments about what fatherhood means to a child more eloquently than I ever could.

Dear Dad,

I've decided to write you a letter of acknowledgment and thanks for your role as my best friend and brother but mostly and most importantly: my Father.

Since a child you have guided and mentored me, been there when I was down (both physically and in spirit) and picked me right back up. You casted away fear and worry out of my mind and heart with your powerful, authoritative voice and deep wisdom. You prayed for me both over the phone and in person. You always want the best for me and have always encouraged me to be great.

You showed me the mindset to aim for the stars. You've taught me almost everything I know (At least the most valuable aspects of me) from walking and talking, riding a bike to being a real Godly man. The camping, hiking and gym conversations and the famous Cape Town- Knysna trip discussions. We have shared our lives and stories and you have even shared your past. We have both learned from the experiences and issues that we had to deal with.

We disagree and have our moments and you taught me that it's healthy and natural. You showed me and we are (in my opinion) an example of a healthy thriving relationship. You introduced me to God and gave me knowledge to form a relationship with him. I have grown into the young man I am today as a result of you and I thank you for it.

There were many hard times that we have been through between: family, Blythe, mom and most importantly was between you and me. The stage where I was living with you and when I wasn't. The time when I moved away. The deeply painful times we had apart. The issues and pain from the farm. The life struggles we had together. They were all really real. You pulled us through them and gave me strength to deal with and process the emotions and pain.

I've never know a more fathered human than me, when I say fathered I mean actually you actually fathering me. You fed me spiritually, emotionally and even taught me wisdom and handed down knowledge. The best part is you continue to do so and I am honoured that all of this has come from you: Craig Louis Wilkinson.

I need to tell you how incredibly grateful I am. There are no words to describe how much these last 18 years of you being my Dad have meant to me now that I can fully grasp what you have done for me. The utter joy and happiness you bring to me are of Devine standards. You can bring this to the rest of the un-fathered world.

You are my father, my role model and my hero. And you will always be.

I love you dad.

Luke

No matter how many times I read this letter, my eyes well up with tears. It was the tipping point that moved me to pursue working with men and fathers full time and to form the non-profit organisation, Father A Nation. My deep desire and prayer is that this book stirs and equips men to become great fathers. Great fathers produce great men and women who lay the foundation of great nations. If we can restore men to fatherhood we can restore society to wholeness.

The focus of this book is on men and fathers. This in no way undermines the crucial role that mothers play in the lives of their children. In fact, I would like to pay tribute to the millions of women throughout the world who are single-handedly holding families together without the emotional, physical and financial support of the men they trusted to be the father of their children. I salute these valiant women and it is for you and your children this book is ultimately written.

It is also written for the millions of dads deeply desiring to be great fathers, struggling with the many challenges of being a man and a dad in this crazy world. Finally, it is written for the men who themselves carry the wounds

THE JOURNEY BEGINS

of not having been fathered well. May these words bring you healing and give you the power to stop the cycle of fatherlessness and begin fathering a whole new world.

PART ONE

FATHERHOOD AND MANHOOD

CHAPTER 1

Fatherhood Matters

"The deepest search in life, it seemed to me, the thing that in one way or another was central to all living was man's search to find a father, not merely the father of his flesh, not merely the lost father of his youth, but the image of a strength and wisdom external to his need and superior to his hunger, to which the belief and power of his own life could be united."
Tom Wolfe

A year after my divorce, my son Luke decided to come and live with me. At the age of 12 he was a big, strong boy, tall and solidly built. He played rugby, loved riding motor bikes and was a real boy in every way. Yet I also noticed a tenderness and vulnerability in him. More than that, there was a cry, a yearning for masculine nurture. He had questions that I needed to answer. His young developing masculine soul needed to draw from a man and that man was me, his father.

For several weeks after moving in with me, Luke would creep into my bed late at night and just hold on to me tightly. It's hard to explain what passed between us during those prolonged, poignant hugs, but it was profound and beautiful. I didn't have to say anything; he was drawing substance from me, almost by osmosis. I was his rock, his anchor. I was the source of masculinity and strength for his developing manhood. No matter what I was experiencing inside, no matter what challenges I was facing, I was Luke's dad and he needed me.

This was a revelation to me. I realised the impact that I as a father could have on my son. I realised that there was a window of opportunity for me to give Luke what he needed and I realised that my willingness and ability to do this would quite possibly be the single biggest influence on his development as a man. I realised then that fatherhood matters deeply, profoundly and undeniably and that a man who becomes a father needs to take this responsibility-laced privilege very seriously.

Being a father and working with human resource development in corporations and socio-economic development in communities has convinced me that of all the roles men play in society, none is more important than the role of father. It is not possible to overemphasise the impact that we have on our children. What we expose them to and what we teach them through our lives, words, actions and interactions helps to form so much more than their world view. It imparts to them their very sense of self, the inner fabric that will equip them for confidence and success or fear and failure.

When Blythe was three years old a vigilant doctor picked up that she had a small hole in one of the walls of her heart and would need corrective surgery. To minimise her trauma, I wanted to be the last one she saw as she fell asleep for the surgery and the first one she saw when she came round. The surgeon allowed me to hold her in my arms as we placed the mask that would put her to sleep over her face. Thanks to modern technology and a good surgeon, the operation was a success.

A few weeks later I overheard Blythe explaining to one of her friends that her heart used to be broken but that her daddy had fixed it. I cried. In her world I was the one who had made everything okay. Emotion welled up in me as I realised what I meant to her as her father. I was the one who could fix anything; her hero. I was the man whose love for her and treatment of her, whose life and actions and words would have the most significant impact on her young heart and mind and soul. My life mattered to her and that made it matter more to me too. I needed to be there for her, to give her my best so that she could grow up to be her best.

Fathers are the most powerful men in their children's lives. What we do with this incredible privilege will shape their beliefs about themselves and the world and largely determine the trajectory of their lives. Every boy longs to be mentored by his father; every girl longs to be adored by her dad. Well-known actress, Halle Berry, is quoted as saying, "I know that I will never find my father in any other man who comes into my life, because it is a void in my life that can only be filled by him".

A father is his daughter's first romance and his son's first hero. He is their first, most important experience of who and what a man is. We set the bar, we are the example, and if we get it right we leave our children with a priceless gift. Impressed into their psyche and souls is the knowledge of a man as a strong, loving sanctuary, a place where there is safety and fun and affirmation. And they will live their lives out of this reservoir of grace and strength. Our sons are more likely to grow up honourable men, treating women with respect and caring for their own families. Our daughters are more likely to grow up as women of stature, making good choices and building strong families of their own.

Being the most important man in someone's life is a privilege that comes with profound responsibilities. Your children will come to you to answer the deepest questions of their hearts. Throughout their developing years they will ask you a thousand times and in a thousand different ways to answer key questions about themselves that no-one else can answer quite like you can. Answer well and you will lay an unshakeable foundation for your children's emotional well-being and character. Answer badly or don't answer at all and you will wound them and quite possibly set them up for a lifetime of emotional struggle.

Failing to answer the deep questions of your son's heart will result in him seeking affirmation for his manhood in countless damaging ways, some involving the abuse of his strength, some involving addictions and some involving withdrawal. Failing to answer the deep questions of your daughter's heart will result in her seeking the answers from other men in ways that will compromise her and almost always lead to heartache.

A few days after Luke was born, I fell in love with him and with fathering him. (It took a few days because – let's be honest – babies are seldom pretty when they first enter the world and as biased as I am, my son was no exception!) I remember being overwhelmed with emotion driving with Luke strapped into his baby seat next to me as I sang along to Bryan Adam's ballad "So if I love you, a little more than I should; please forgive me I know not what I do". No-one had warned me of the depth of emotion that I would experience for my young boy. A new love had been born, one greater than anything I could have anticipated. What was different about this love was that the object of it was a vulnerable life entirely incapable of surviving by itself.

I felt such a sense of responsibility that my survival instinct increased tenfold. Suddenly all the crazy things that I had always been prone to do, such as leaping out of a perfectly functioning plane or roaring down a wild river in a flimsy raft, took on a whole new perspective as my need to stay alive and well to look after my son superseded all else.

Fatherhood has made me more vulnerable than any other experience. It has humbled me, healed me and transformed me. It has brought me tears of joy on more occasions than I can remember; sleepless nights, worry, fear and pride. It has given me a reason to live when times have been tough; it has inspired me to live right when I was tempted to lose my bearings.

I certainly haven't got it all right. Like every father before me and every one still to come, I entered fatherhood as a flawed and wounded man. Yet fatherhood offered me the opportunity and inspiration to look in the mirror and see what I might otherwise never have seen. It gave me the reason I needed to change what needed to change. It made me realise what I had not received growing up and the hurt and lack that this had caused, and it inspired me to find healing for myself so that I could give my children all that they needed from me.

When Luke turned 13 I conducted a rites of passage ceremony for him. I asked eight men whom I respected as fathers and role models to participate. It was a profoundly beautiful weekend and everyone was moved by the experience. What struck me most though was not the impact that it had on my son but the effect that it had on the men who were involved. Almost every one of them confided afterwards that in some way or another the experience had highlighted what they had not received from their fathers. There was a distant longing, a dull pain that had resurfaced as they participated in the sacred impartation of the masculine by the masculine. It was a longing for what their fathers had not given them as they grew up.

Since then I have become increasingly aware of the impact that fathers have on the lives of their children and how much damage they can do if they fail to father well. It is astounding how many adults carry hurt from their relationship with their fathers. Many are not consciously aware of it, but most men and women carry in their hearts a wound from their father. Some of these wounds are blatant and debilitating, such as when physical or sexual abuse has taken place, but most are subtle, resulting from fathers who were present in body but not effectively engaged in their children's lives. Very few men set out to deliberately harm their children, yet most men fail to give their children all they need. They wound their children by what they fail to do right more than what they succeed in doing wrong.

The wounds inflicted by passive fathers don't destroy but they damage. They affect the ability of their children to be fully alive. They erode their self-esteem and subtly but significantly affect the important life choices they make as adults. The reality is that every father influences the lives of his children forever. That's a given. Whether this impact is for good or for harm is the choice every father has to make.

Shortly after a friend of mine started working with male prisoners he was inundated with requests from the inmates for cards to give to their mothers on the upcoming Mother's Day. He happily obliged and a month or so later decided to pre-empt the requests for Father's Day cards by buying them before being asked. To his shock and dismay, not one of the men who had asked for a card for their mother asked for one for their father. When he questioned the men, almost all said that they either did not know their father or were estranged from him. What a graphic demonstration of the wounds absent fathers inflict on their sons.

Research on the social implications of absent or passive fathers reveals some frightening facts. The statistical link between absent or abusive fathers and every category of emotional and social dysfunction is direct and undeniable. Young people who grow up with absent fathers are at significantly greater risk of falling into substance abuse, promiscuity, early pregnancy, abuse, violence and crime. The greatest predictor of social pathology in children is fatherlessness, greater even than poverty. In his book *Fatherless Generation* (Zondervan) John

DAD

Sowers claims, "The most reliable predictor for gang activity and youth violence is neither social class nor race or education but fatherlessness."

In *Fatherless America* (Basic Books) David Blankenhorn says, "It is no exaggeration to say that fatherlessness is the most harmful demographic trend of this generation. It is the engine driving our most urgent social problems". I am convinced that the damage to humanity caused by the epidemic of unfathered men and women is far greater than the damage caused by war and disease combined.

A look at the childhood of some of the worst dictators in history bears stark testimony to this. Joseph Stalin's father was a violent alcoholic who beat him and his mother relentlessly. Adolf Hitler's father abused him physically and died when Hitler was 14 years old. Saddam Hussein was fatherless from birth. Fathers matter. They impact their children's lives profoundly, for good or for bad.

It's easy to view the scourge of fatherlessness as something that only affects people from poor or dysfunctional communities. The reality is that the damage done by absent or abusive fathers cuts across all communities. Whether they are rich or poor, educated or not, and regardless of culture or ethnicity, children need actively engaged fathers. When fathers are absent children are wounded. It's as simple as that. And a father does not need to live apart from his children to be absent. Many fathers live in the same house as their children but are effectively absent in mind and heart.

It is entirely possible to grow up in a household with two

parents yet still have an orphaned heart. Someone aptly said that it's hard to know which is more painful: a father that you've never seen and never known or a father that you've seen and never known. Passive fathers are effectively absent fathers and their children walk with those who are fatherless.

To use the analogy of producing a film, there is no body double or understudy for the role of father. On the birth of your child you landed the all-important role of father, producer, actor, director and script writer. And if you don't set the stage and edit the script for the unfolding story of your child's life, others will, and the epic that results may not be the grand adventure you hoped for but a dangerous thriller or – even worse – a bland, B-grade story played in a forlorn and forgotten bug house.

Dramatic as this may sound, true fatherhood requires serious intent and consistent action. Being a great father doesn't just happen. It takes a deliberate commitment. True fatherhood cannot be outsourced or delegated; it must be handled personally. Just as a safe can only be opened by the key specifically designed for it, you as a father hold the key to unlock the potential in your child's life.

The world is crying out for men who will step up to the plate and be great fathers. Every father has a window of opportunity to provide input into his children's lives. And like most windows of opportunity, it eventually closes. The more input a father makes into his children's younger years, the greater will be his influence in their later years. Too many fathers wake up late and try to discipline a teenager who is already showing signs of bad behaviour. Fathers need to get involved immediately and stay involved for the rest of their lives.

Fatherhood offers a chance for men to lay foundations of self-belief and conscious, principled behaviour that will affect not only the lives of their own children but generations to come. Fatherhood also offers a chance to mess up monumentally.

This book is a call to men to be great fathers. Not perfect fathers, for there is no such thing, but great fathers. Every man has the potential to be a great father and every child deserves to have one. The wonderful thing about being a dad is that we all get to be a hero. Of course, this means that we have to live up to some pretty high expectations. But that's okay, because every dad has it in him to be a hero to his children. My hope is that this book will show you how to be that hero, how to be the man that sets up life for your children, who imparts to them all they need to fly. They deserve it and so do you.

CHAPTER 2

Masculinity Under Fire

"We (modern society) make men without chests and expect of them virtue and enterprise. We laugh at honor and are shocked to find traitors in our midst. We castrate and bid the geldings be fruitful."
C.S. Lewis

At the heart of fatherhood is masculinity. Yet we live in a world in which the definition and perception of masculinity is mired in confusion and negativity. What is a true man? The media image of masculinity has degenerated to the point where it is more often reviled than revered. Men are portrayed as everything from emotionally incompetent layabouts to posers and philanderers.

Sadly, much of the negative press men have received in the last few years has been justified. Men are increasingly losing the plot, failing to stand up and embrace their responsibilities. Women are asking "where are all the good men?" Young men are asking "where are the mentors and role models?" More and more books and articles are being written about the crisis of masculinity. Our belief as a society in the value of masculinity has waned and unfortunately our experience of men has done at least as much to confirm as belie this belief.

Not long ago the typical man was seen as a strong and proud figure. He worked hard, lived with integrity, was chivalrous and had strong family values. He was a good provider and was committed to his wife and children. His role in society and at home was very clear. He could be trusted and relied upon. Fast forward to today and society's perception of masculinity and the role of men is negative and confused.

Where is the image of true masculinity to be found? Is it in the round-house kick of Chuck Norris or in the decaf latte of the tame metrosexual? Is masculinity epitomised by the pot-bellied, middle aged, suburban man in front of the sports channel sipping beer and yelling advice to a team of men he has never met, or by the suave wall-street broker in a pin-striped suit? Does the tough inner city gang member embody masculinity or the outdoor man hiking through the wilderness? The image of true masculinity is as varied as the number of people you ask.

In the midst of this masculine identity crisis it must be said that true masculinity is a powerful and positive force for good. A man who is truly masculine embraces responsibility and does all in his power to love, honour, protect and provide for his family and loved ones. He lives with integrity, motivated by conviction, not comfort or convenience. He never takes what is not his but understands that reward comes from hard work and commitment. He has the courage to face the consequences of his actions.

True masculinity is not determined by how much physical

strength a man has but rather the strength of his character. It is not a matter of how much wealth or power a man has but what he does with the wealth and power that he does have. A truly masculine man is not one who boasts of many conquests but one who keeps his commitment to one woman. True masculinity is humble. It is unafraid to apologise and admit wrong. It is not about dominance but service; it is seen in the doing, not the saying.

A truly masculine man is courageous, unyielding in the face of danger and uncompromising in his convictions, but to his loved ones he is a source of tenderness and a place of safety. True masculinity is virtuous and noble, a beautiful gift to the man who possesses it and to the people he loves.

If this is true masculinity, what on earth has gone wrong and where are all the truly masculine men? Why do so few men get it right? Why are great marriages the exception rather than the norm? Why are so many children growing up in homes with absent or abusive fathers? Why are more men not stepping up to the plate and using their strength and masculinity to fight for their families and live virtuous lives driven by noble purpose?

I believe there are two main reasons. The first is a misconception about what true masculinity is and the second is the wound to their masculinity that most men carry.

Misconstrued notions about what manhood is drive many of the damaging behaviours of men. These notions are often culture specific but generally they follow the same theme: men who are bigger, stronger, faster, wealthier, cooler, sleep with more women, and so on, are real men. Men who buy into such ill-conceived concepts of masculinity spend the rest of their lives posing and posturing, trying to match up to what their image of what a real man is. They strive to be bigger, stronger, faster, cooler than they really are, believing that who they are is not man enough. And the sad thing is that the men they are posing for are doing the same thing. It's a great deception and by buying into false notions about what a real man is we lose our authenticity and sell ourselves terribly short.

I remember driving into Luke's school to collect him one afternoon. It was a good school with a large number of fairly well-off parents. On this particular day my car was in for service and I had borrowed an old, clapped out run-around for the day. As I drove on to the campus I saw some of the other parents driving towards the exit. I'm embarrassed to say that I ducked down and covered my face so they wouldn't see me driving a beaten-up old car. How foolish! I had fallen into the trap of defining and valuing myself by the car I drove and not the man I am.

In his book, *Principle Centred Leadership* (Free Press), Steven Covey talks about how we as a society have shifted from valuing character and values to valuing image and personality. Not too long ago a man was judged by the strength of his character. Character and integrity mattered more than wealth and status. A man would choose principle over possessions any day of the week. His value was in his name and his word. Covey called this the character ethic. Today we value status, money, pleasure and comfort. Our consciences are guided by convenience not conviction. This Covey called the personality ethic.

The personality ethic puts more stock in what you can see on the outside than what is held on the inside. As long as we can create an image of wealth or power or youth or whatever else it is that the people around us value, we are okay. So men put a great deal of energy into creating an acceptable self which they present to the world. Unfortunately it is very often a false self. The famous basketball coach John Wooden put it well when he said, "Be more concerned with your character than your reputation, because your character is what you really are, while your reputation is merely what others think you are."

When we value image above character we devalue and compromise ourselves. We start putting the highest value on the things that actually matter the least; our image becomes our God and we lose sight of what our lives are truly all about. There is a reason the trappings of wealth are called that; they trap. But materialism is just one of the many traps that ensnare men in their quest to live up to society's message about what a real man is. By defining ourselves by what we do, what we own or what other people think of us, we lose ourselves to the whims and wishes of a fickle and skin deep societal arbiter.

True masculinity requires the courage to live authentically, to measure our strength and our worth by who we are, not on what we have and on what others say about us. Gandhi summed it up perfectly when he said, "Manliness consists not in bluff, bravado or loneliness. It consists in daring to do the right thing and facing consequences whether it is in matters social, political or other. It consists in deeds not words."

The second reason why men are getting it wrong on such

a large scale is that their own masculinity is wounded. In his book, *Wild at Heart* (Thomas Nelson) John Eldredge says, "Every boy, in his journey to become a man, takes an arrow in the centre of his heart, in the place of his strength. Because the wound is rarely discussed and even more rarely healed, every man carries a wound. And the wound is nearly always given by his father."

How does this wounding take place? For a boy's masculine soul to function as it should, there are three fundamental questions that need to be answered by his father as he grows up: who am I, do I matter and do I have what it takes? The first relates to identity, the second to validity and the third to self-belief. These questions of identity and validity that lead to self-belief are directed at a boy's father and no-one else can answer as effectively as he can.

Nothing is more important in a boy's formative years than having these questions answered by his father. And every father, whether he knows it or not, answers; for good or for harm. By their silence, passive or absent fathers answer with; "you don't matter, I don't care". Abusive fathers answer in a brutally negative way by directly attacking their son's developing, still vulnerable masculine soul. Their message is: "you're worthless, you don't count". When a father fails to answer or answers badly, his son will grow up with a wound at the core of his masculine soul.

The number of ways fathers inflict wounds on the masculine souls of their sons is endless. A boy who waits in vain for his dad to come home and play with him night after night gets the message from his father that he is not important; he doesn't matter. A boy who is told by his father not to be stupid, or that he is clumsy, or slow, or lazy, or any number of seemingly harmless labels that dads put on their sons, will take it to heart and grow up believing what his father told him. A boy who is told not to be a cry baby will lock his emotions in a hard corner of his heart and will grow up with the message that what he feels doesn't matter.

Most fathers are largely unaware of the damage they are doing to their children. It happens as part of a self-perpetuating cycle. Wounded son grows up to be wounded father who out of his hurt wounds his son, and so it continues until a conscious and courageous man breaks the cycle by dealing with his wound and choosing to father well.

Men whose fathers have answered their questions about identity and validity well grow up strong and secure in their manhood. They have no need to prove themselves in inappropriate ways. They are able to offer their strength to a woman and love her with respect and loyalty. They are able to live lives of conviction and purpose, not succumbing to the shallow pursuit of image, comfort and macho-ism.

Men whose fathers fail to answer their masculinity questions grow up wounded. They carry this wound into manhood and it affects everything they do. Wounded men become men that wound. Men whose masculinity has been wounded respond by becoming passive or aggressive, or sometimes a strange mix of both. A man can be passive at home and aggressive at work, displayed by his absence from home life and driving ambition at work. Or else a man may present a kind and agreeable persona at work and become a controlling tyrant at home.

Passive men generally retreat, living lives of silent mediocrity, not stepping up to the plate as a man because they either don't know what it means or they don't believe they have what it takes. Aggressive men come out swinging, on a mission to prove that they really are men. Both hide behind façades, fearing discovery of who they really are. And both are likely to escape into addictions of various kinds; some socially acceptable like working or training obsessively, others less so, like watching pornography or abusing substances. All these activities are designed to anaesthetise the pain and find some affirmation of their masculinity.

In his book, *Money, Sex & Power* (Hodder & Stoughton) Author Richard Foster shows how money, sex and power are the three areas in which men struggle and fall most. Wounded men, whether passive or aggressive, will inevitably struggle with compulsive behaviour in one or all of these areas. In the area of sex it will manifest in such ways as sexual addiction, compulsive masturbation, affairs, lust or pornography. If the area of struggle is power it will display itself in the need to control, driving ambition, super-competitiveness and sometimes sexual abuse. In the case of money the evidence will be an obsession with material possessions, keeping up with the Joneses and valuing wealth above all else. Men often struggle in all three of these areas. The extent of the wound will determine the extent of the struggle.

Fundamental to the nature of masculinity is that it cannot

MASCULINITY UNDER FIRE

simply be taught. It needs to be imparted. And this impartation must come from a man or men. It takes masculinity to impart masculinity. For centuries in different cultures and communities around the world men would conduct rites of passage programmes in which a boy would leave the comfort of his mother's embrace for a time and be initiated into the company of men. This ritual involved a number of key elements; a forsaking of the things of childhood, a test of strength and character, impartation of age old wisdom by a company of men and finally the acceptance and blessing of men who had themselves walked the journey from boyhood to manhood. Young men emerged from this process with a clear understanding of what it was to be a man. They held themselves with pride, secure in the knowledge that they now walked as a man among men.

In today's world not only is the practice of initiating boys into manhood almost non-existent, but men largely expect the development of their son's masculine soul to happen by default. And in the bewildering and ill-defined landscape of today's perception of masculinity, it's no wonder that men grow up with a crisis of their masculine identity.

Moms play a crucial role in the lives of their children and many are valiantly trying to fill the gap left by passive or absent fathers, but there are certain things they cannot do. So many mothers who pour their lives into raising their children in the absence of the fathers are deeply hurt when their teenage boys start to resent them. They struggle to discipline them as they take out their frustration and hunger for a father in rebellion against their mothers. What is actually pain from an absent father comes out as anger towards a present mother, while a deep longing remains for the man who fathered them. Moms may fuss over their boys and call them "sweetheart". The endearment is beautiful and needed, but it's not enough; there are things they need to hear from their fathers.

Boys need someone to test their strength against, someone who will call them "tiger" and play rough with them. When Luke was about to turn 11, I asked him what he wanted to do for his birthday party. The list of activities he chose was telling: play rugby, have an arm-wrestling competition, a wrestling match between me and all of his friends (at the same time!), let off some firecrackers, blow something up, cook meat over a fire, and then to crown it all, stay up the whole night playing TV games. We did it all. It was mayhem, but it was wonderful. The testosterone was palpable. There was impartation, the younger men pitting their strength against the older, exploring their own strength and ability, growing in masculinity. Boys need this in some form or another from their fathers and other older men and those who don't get it are inevitably wounded.

For men with wounded masculinity, life is a constant quest to find identity and validation and to prove that they have what it takes. Fuel this quest with some of the popular misconceptions about what a real man is and you have a recipe for disaster and an explanation for almost all of the strange behaviour of the male species. Why else would a man drink himself senseless and then perform all manner of strange and dangerous exploits to prove and impress? Why would a man run off with a woman

20 years his junior and in one fell swoop destroy his family and reputation?

At the core of all this irrational behaviour is a deep, secret fear that they are not quite adequate as men. Whether in the bar or boardroom, battlefield or bedroom, men fight to prove they are the real deal. And what gets lost in the madness is the strength and beauty of the true masculine soul. The liberating truth is that you don't have to play the man to be the man. You are the man, and so much more so, if you don't have a constant need to prove it.

How does this affect our ability to father? Both passive and aggressive fathers are damaging to children. The abusive man takes the gift of his strength and misuses it to dominate and damage. Whether physical or sexual, verbal or psychological, abuse in any form is grounded in a distorted view of masculinity and perpetrated by very wounded men. Some forms of abuse can be subtle, like sarcasm and cutting remarks; some forms can appear passive, like sulking and withdrawing. The effect of all abuse is to destroy the self-esteem and identity of the victim. It's tragic to think that the beautiful gift of strength that men have been given can bring harm to the very lives they are tasked to protect.

Fortunately, most men do not knowingly and deliberately harm their children. But while relatively few fathers use their strength to abuse their children, most are in some way or another guilty of failing to use their strength to provide their children with all they need from a father. They wound by being passive. Passivity is the opposite of masculinity. Femininity complements masculinity; passivity makes a mockery of it. By his silence, absence or indifference, the passive man gives the message to his children that they don't matter. Work, sport, television, leisure or (in the case of a divorced man) a new woman, are all given more importance than them. He entrusts the education of his children in the ways and values of life to the media and to his children's peers.

Such a dereliction of duty has disastrous results. A passive man wreaks silent havoc in the lives of his children. They are starved of vital emotional and spiritual nutrients and unless they find an alternative source they will be wounded and stunted in their own growth.

Absent fathers are the ultimate in passivity. Those who are simply not around – other than for valid reasons, and there are some – have violated the sacred trust of fatherhood. They have abdicated their masculinity. I would go as far as saying that if there is a young life out there falling asleep crying for his dad, and you are that dad, you have lost the right to call yourself a man. Children need their dads. It is unnatural and unmanly for a dad to abandon his children.

Boys and girls need fathers who know who they are, fathers who will impart to them the emotional and spiritual building blocks they need to build a great life. No man in good conscience would knowingly and willingly neglect his duties to his children, yet many men are held back in their ability to father because of their own impoverished understanding of fatherhood and the wounds they carry. Having picked up this book and read to this point, you are clearly a man who wants to be a good father. And being a true father starts with being a true man.

CHAPTER 3

Manning Up

One night a father overheard his son pray: "Dear God, make me the kind of man my Daddy is". Later that night, the Father prayed, "Dear God, Make me the kind of man my son wants me to be".
Author Unknown

"Our children will listen to our way and not what we say." This quote from an unknown source sums up one of the greatest challenges of being a father. Our children receive far more from what they see us do than what they hear us say. What we teach them must come from who we are as men, not what our heads tell us is the right thing. No matter what we say to our children, the way we live our lives will ultimately be their greatest teacher.

No matter how hard we may try to hide it, whatever is in our hearts will reflect in the way we live. Whether love or bitterness, anger or peace, the content of our souls spills out into the conduct of our lives. And nowhere is this more evident than in our families. It's possible to pull the wool over the world's eyes by presenting an image that is different from what we hold inside, but our families always see the truth. Because your wife and children are so close to you, sooner or later they will pick up on the real you. There is no escaping it.

As a father what you impart to your children comes from your core, the real you. The simple reality is we cannot give to our children what we don't have within us to give; and what we do have within us, both good and bad, will be imparted in some way to our children. Because of this, not only is our conduct important to the quality of our fatherhood but so is our own inner life.

The way we live speaks louder than anything we say.

We can only impart to our children what we have inside us to impart.

What we have inside us, both good and bad, will be imparted to our children.

These are three crucial and inescapable realities every man serious about fatherhood needs to embrace. They present a great challenge but also a great opportunity for personal transformation and growth. It means that not only do we need to ensure that the way we live our lives reflects what we want to teach our children, but what's inside us is worth passing on to our children. This requires a serious "manning up".

I once lectured in a subject that I had not previously studied and I remember anxious nights spent learning the material that I would have to teach with authority the very next day.

Fatherhood often feels that way. What Luke and Blythe have asked of me has often highlighted what I never received myself. Often what we are called on to impart to our children highlights the very thing we ourselves lack and the wounds that we carry. Yet rather than being a disaster this creates an opportunity to step up to the plate and be and become a man as we nurture and grow a boy to become a man and a girl to become a woman.

The first courageous step we need to take in manning up to become a great father is to deal with our own masculine wound. Many who read this will immediately respond with the thought, "This doesn't apply to me. Perhaps I should skip to the next section". Don't be so hasty. If you are one of the rare and fortunate men who had a near perfect father and childhood you may be close to being able to say, "I know who I am and what I am worth. My validity as a man is in no doubt; I am completely authentic in all I say and do. If my thoughts and heart were an open book to my family and the world I would fear no embarrassment, for I have nothing to hide. The person I present to the world in every circumstance is the real me, without any posturing. I carry no anger, no regrets about what could have been. I am content with who and what I am and where I am going, with the kind of man, father, and husband I am and I know my wife and children would say the same about me".

If you can say all this with honesty and conviction then by all means skip to the next chapter. Very few men can. It's pretty safe to say that all men have some level of woundedness in their masculine souls and if we are serious about the business of manhood and fatherhood we need to be honest enough to admit it and brave enough to deal with it. As men we tend to cover up our wounds and just get on with life. After years of covering up and burying our wounds deeply in our psyche we are not even aware that we carry a wound.

But our woundedness drives our behaviour in ways that are often unconscious. Fathers with wounded masculinity either perpetuate the wounds they received from their own fathers or overcompensate in the other extreme. Fathers trying to live out their unrealised dreams vicariously through their children are wounded and are wounding their children. Fathers who set no boundaries because their own fathers were disciplinarians are wounding their children. Fathers who relentlessly pursue wealth and success at the expense of time with their family are wounded and are wounding their children. Fathers who escape into addictions like pornography, alcohol or work are wounded and are wounding their children.

I entered fatherhood a wounded man. My sense of identity was scattered, my belief in self was shaky at best. And so I did what men do so well: I played the man, or at least what I believed the man ought to be. My soul was not whole and so it sought comfort and validation and solace in ways that compromised me and those who I loved and who relied on me. I began to see that unless I received healing for my own masculine soul, any deficiencies, insecurities and hurts that I had would so influence the way that I fathered that I would run the risk of passing them on to my children.

A long journey of healing and re-fathering began in my life. There have been casualties along the way: a failed marriage, lost opportunities, dysfunctional behaviour, the pain of living in a different city to my children, the expense of constant travelling to be with them, and the inevitable heartache of separation. Divorce is undeniably painful for children and it's both challenging and less than ideal to father children who are spending time in two different households.

Healing our masculine wound requires intentionality, time and help. It does not happen by default, nor does it happen overnight, and it certainly will not take place in a vacuum. My own healing and re-fathering has been (and continues to be) a deliberate and increasingly conscious process. I have read extensively, prayed much, attended countless workshops, sat through counselling sessions, talked with friends, seen things in myself I hated to see, and been through times of near despair. But as tough as it has been, it has also been a beautiful, life-changing journey.

The second courageous step in manning up to be a great father is to live an authentic masculine life. This will require you to look at what true masculinity is, to assess your own life, and to make the changes needed for you to live with authentic masculinity. Once again this is easier said than done and is a journey requiring commitment and dedication. But it is worth every ounce of effort you put in; for your children and for yourself.

All men have three basic yearnings: purpose, adventure and romance. John Elldredge puts it beautifully in his book *Wild at*

Heart when he writes that every masculine soul needs a battle to fight, an adventure to live and a beauty to rescue. As men we come alive when our souls find expression in these three areas. If you have any doubt, just watch boys play. I've seen parents with a strong conviction about pacifism try to keep toy guns from their sons. It doesn't work. They carve guns out of chunks of wood and turn ordinary household implements into weapons of mass destruction. Boys are not content to simply ride a bicycle; they have to do it with no hands and then standing up and then build higher and higher ramps to fly off. Battle and adventure are embedded in the masculine soul and need to find expression.

Unfortunately, in today's sanitised and digitalised world, battles and adventure are not easy to come by. And in our overly eroticised society, romance has largely been reduced to the physical act of sex. What used to be love's consummation is now sold as its conception. Today most men attempt to satisfy their need for battle, adventure and romance by living vicariously through others or in the playground of virtual reality.

We sit on our couches week after week watching our favourite team do battle against the opposition on the sports field. We yearn for a noble cause, a battle to fight. Because we don't have one of our own, we identify ourselves with a sports team. We feel elated when they win and depressed when they lose. We somehow link our masculine validity to the success of the team we support. Or we spend countless hours playing computer games, battling aliens or monsters in some digital never-never land. It's sad and it's lonely because it's not the real thing.

Our quest for romance is often even more sad and lonely. Porn addiction has reached almost epidemic proportions. Men are spending an ever-increasing amount of time in front of their computer screens trawling porn sites, seeking a distorted form of the romance our masculine souls crave. We've been seduced by a lie, believing that somehow millions of pixels on a computer screen can satisfy our soul's cry for romance and beauty. It's a deadly trap and one that millions of men are battling to escape. Pornography destroys intimacy because no woman can ever live up to the images of erotic perfection it so brazenly displays. And even if they do, it won't last because in the fantasy world of digitised sex, a new, younger, slimmer, sexier woman is just a click away.

None of this works to satisfy the masculine soul because none of it is real. All it does is feed growing addictions, cause more frustration and erode our masculinity. Instead of being virtuous our lives become virtual. What is the way out of this futile maze? Is it possible to find fulfilment for the masculine soul and live as a true man in this modern world?

The answer is a resounding yes! When a man understands his masculine soul and what drives it, confusion about his role and identity gives way to a deep sense of conviction and purpose and he is able to embrace his masculinity with gratitude and joy. He is able to break away from the sterile strictures and digital distractions of modern living and find purpose, adventure and true romance.

DAD

The richest and most important source of battle, adventure and romance for a man is found in his own family. A father's most important fight is for his children; to ensure that they are safe, educated, loved and provided for. To do this well a man will need to draw on all the qualities of true masculinity. It doesn't come easily; as resilient as children are, they are also fragile and complex beings who grow up in a world full of potential danger. Raising children well is a noble purpose and a battle worth fighting.

A man's most challenging and rewarding romance is a lifelong commitment to one woman. It is something over fifty per cent of men fail in. To succeed in this noble challenge, a man will need to draw deeply on the virtues and strengths of true masculinity. There will be dragons to slay, but they won't be the ones you read about in fairy tales. Just as no man reached manhood unscathed by his childhood, women bear their own wounds. And the woman who mothers your child will be no exception. She will carry her wounds and scars into your relationship and as her knight in shining armour you will have to rescue her from them by walking with her in love and truth through her own healing process. This is true romance. And it is found in your own home.

And while you are raising your children and romancing your wife there is purpose to be found and adventure to be lived outside the home too. (There is also romance, but it's false, and the only way to deal with that is to flee!) The best way to satisfy the cry of the masculine soul for purpose is to find it and live it. Men are crying out for lives that matter, lives that have purpose. As an illustration of that, Rick Warren's book, *The*

Purpose Driven Life (Zondervan), is the bestselling nonfiction hardback in history!

Men lose their masculine fire when their only purpose in life is to pay the bills. But there is no need to fall into this treadmill-shaped trap. In almost every sphere of society there are noble causes to put your heart into and fight and, in so doing, satisfy the cry of your masculine soul for purpose and adventure. One of the great benefits of finding a cause worth fighting for is that it will undoubtedly come with its share of adventure.

Adventure itself is not difficult to find. It simply requires breaking routine, getting off the couch, getting out from in front of the television or computer screen and leaving the comfort and convenience of the house. What constitutes adventure differs from person to person. The important thing is not to fall into a trap of living the same old life, year after year. Many people who claim to have 30 years of experience actually only have one year, repeated 30 times over.

The power and importance of making a determined decision to find healing for your masculine wound and to live with authentic masculinity cannot be overstated. It will change your life and the lives of those you love forever. It will start you on the adventure of a lifetime and a journey of discovery from which you will never look back. It will set you and your family up for lives of significance and meaning.

Fatherhood starts with me. It starts with me dealing with my issues, developing an understanding of what it is to be true man, having the wisdom to identify and the courage to discard the misconceptions that popular media and sometimes my own culture perpetuate about manhood. It starts with me manning up to live with authentic masculinity. This is a journey and not an event. While we are busy manning up, we need to carry on with the all-important task of fathering our children. It is a parallel process learning to become a whole and true man while raising our sons and daughters to themselves become whole and true men and women.

The word "father" is a noun, but it is also, more importantly, a verb. A man does not earn the title simply by the birth of his child but by countless acts of fathering from the day his child is born till the day he breathes his last. These acts of fathering I have called dadverbs. The next section of this book deals with 12 key dadverbs that every dad needs to make an integral part of raising his children.

PART TWO

FATHERHOOD IN ACTION

CHAPTER 4

Call Out

"To the world you might be one person, but to one person you might be the world."
Bill Wilson

One of the primary roles of a father is to call out the identity of his son or daughter. The wide-eyed, unstated question of both boys and girls to their father is, who am I, where do I come from, what am I made of? Answering well takes their whole childhood and the very best of you. Many fathers are either unaware of the question and end up ignoring it altogether or try to mould their children into what they would like them to be.

One of the greatest longings we all have is to be truly seen, truly known. People often fall in love with the first person who really "gets them", even if the person is not right in most other ways. It is a universal soul cry and it is one that every father needs to respond to. Thus the first dadverb is to **see.**

William Shakespeare said that "It is a wise father that knows his own child". A good father makes it a mission to discover the essence of his son or his daughter. He hears and sees. He listens to his children's words, their body language, their behaviour, what their eyes are saying. He knows them. He knows what makes his daughter's heart come alive, what her favourite colour is, her fears, passions, likes, dislikes. He knows what excites his son, what will make him get up early in the morning raring to go.

Most of us are guilty of being more concerned with getting our own point across than listening to what the other person is saying. There is great wisdom in "seeking first to understand before being understood" as Steven Covey says in his inspiring book, *The Seven Habits of Highly Effective People* (Simon & Schuster). It is so important to get this right with our children. It means putting listening above telling, seeing above being seen and it does not come naturally for most men.

Much of the angst of teenage years is a result of young people not feeling understood. Much of the frustration and rebellion we experience from our children is a direct result of us as fathers just not "getting them". If you make it a habit from when your children are still very young to listen to them, hear them and understand them you will greatly reduce the odds of them becoming angry, rebellious teenagers.

I have been guilty on many occasions of not hearing my children. I remember one conversation I had with Luke in which we disagreed quite strongly. Not long into the discussion he started to withdraw and become quiet and I noticed that he had tears in his eyes. I asked him what was wrong and after some prodding I realised that I had been overriding him with my view and had not been listening to him and allowing him to get his point across. He was frustrated and upset, and it was my fault.

As a father it is easy to dominate. You are bigger, stronger and have more authority. I had to learn to keep quiet, holding back my own strong opinion while allowing Luke to express himself fully. This is the starting point of truly understanding your child. Children don't always have the words and the reference points to clearly articulate what they want to say and so it is often easy to discount what they are saying and override it with stronger arguments.

Instead of doing this we need to help them articulate and frame what they are saying, we need to take time to really get into their heads and hearts and listen and hear. We need to let them know that what they feel and think matters and help them to express it and then feed it back to them in a way that makes sense to them and us.

When a child is quiet or frustrated it often means that they don't feel seen or heard. A father must make it a mission to hear and understand, to see and acknowledge. Knowing your child lets them know that they matter, that what they think and feel is important. It affirms and validates them. It gives credence to who they are and creates in them the confidence to be themselves.

An important part of seeing your child is to notice what they are doing and take time to let them know that you do. I told the story in an earlier chapter about Luke's 11th birthday party. While he and his friends were doing their best to rough me up and destroy the neighbourhood, Blythe had a few of her own friends around and they were playing a somewhat different game. They had climbed into her mom's wardrobe and were parading around in a variety of outfits, tottering about in high heels way too large for their feet.

I took some time out from the testosterone-fuelled mayhem to acknowledge her and tell her how beautiful she looked. We ended up doing an impromptu photo shoot. Blythe needed to be seen by her dad but what she wanted me to see was very different from what her brother wanted me to see. She needed me to see that she was beautiful. And I did. And I told her. And she glowed.

It is very difficult to see someone else if you have not first seen yourself and so once again, the parallel journey of fathering requires that we as men get in touch with who we are so that we can better see and understand who our children are. There is a beautiful scene in the movie *Chariots of Fire* when Eric Liddell, a preacher and an athlete, is being berated by his sister for putting his running above preaching. She tells him that "God made you to preach". His inspiring reply was "yes, but He also made me fast, and when I run I feel His pleasure".

This is the question we as men need to ask ourselves: what is our running? What is that thing or things that when I do them I feel God's pleasure? This is the essence of who we are. We need to discover it and live it and we need to help our children discover their running too. What a great gift that is to them, to let them know that we see them and what we see is good. Your children need to be seen; be the one who sees them. If you don't, they will find someone who does, and you may not like who they find.

This brings us to the next important dadverb and that is to **identify.** Each child has a unique identity; a combination of personality traits, talents and passions that combine to equip them for their life purpose. It's your duty as a father to help them discover what their skill set is and how this melds with their heart's great passion to form their unique identity.

As fathers we need to identify who our children are, what their unique gifts and talents, likes and dislikes are. Most of us project on to our children in some way what we would like them to be and so restrict our ability to truly see them as they are, rather than how we would like them to be. We see our children as a reflection of ourselves. Their success represents our success. As a result, many fathers live out their ambitions and unfulfilled desires through their sons.

Your child may have an identity and purpose which is completely different from yours. It takes a big man to recognise in his son something fundamentally different from himself, to connect with this, love and accept it and to nurture it. A man who is a sports fanatic will often have a hard time accepting a son who is more academically inclined, with no interest in sport. It is crucial, however, that he recognises who his son is and doesn't project what he would like his son to be.

Wanting our children to be something that they are not, something that we want for them and that is not necessarily what they want for themselves, is a rejection of who they are and will seriously damage their self-esteem.

This point is highlighted in the tragic story in the film, *Dead Poet's Society.* The son was passionate about drama and yet as hard as he tried he could not get his father's approval. His father demanded that his son become a corporate man. Haunted by his father's rejection of who he was at his very core and unable to subvert his essence to be something that he truly was not, the son eventually took his own life.

Once you make the effort to truly discover who and what your child is, it's amazing what you will find. Blythe is many things: tomboy, budding model, writer and social activist, athlete, compassionate nurturer, loving daughter, loyal sister, deep thinker, faithful friend, sensitive soul, brave adventurer. For her to fully develop into all God created her to be she needs to explore the many facets that make up who she is and she needs me as her father to create the environment and opportunities in which to do so.

One of the ways of helping your children discover who they are is by exposing them to as many different opportunities and experiences as you can. This means taking them away from the TV set, and the Play-station, getting them to step away from whatever form of social networking they are engaged in and exposing them to such diverse activities as theatre, hiking, travel, museums. Through exposure to different experiences they will discover what they like and don't like and, with luck, even uncover a lifelong passion.

It's no great revelation to state that we are all different. I love the outdoors. Hiking through a forest or up a mountain with my family is one of my all-time favourite activities. Luke also loves hiking and we often head out into the hills together. Blythe, on the other hand, does not; in fact, she feels quite strongly about not wanting to hike (hopefully not due to an enforced overexposure from a young age by her hike-happy dad!). Her view is that if you can drive somewhere, why walk? As much as I want her to come hiking with me, it is just not her thing and that is absolutely fine.

Blythe loves dancing and has done ballet, hip hop and ballroom lessons. Luke loves motor cross biking. I much prefer getting on a mountain bike and cycling. Luke and Blythe discovered these and many other interests, likes and dislikes through exposure to them. Had they spent their childhood glued to the TV or lost in a social networking maze, they may never have discovered some of their great passions. As fathers we need to create experiences for our children that help them discover who they are, what they like and don't like. This will often take them out of their comfort zones but that is a good thing as it will grow and stretch them as they discover who and what they are.

Another way of effectively identifying your children is to actively observe and feed back to them what you see. When Blythe was just over two years old I spotted her reaching out curiously towards a red hot heater. I quickly said to her, "Don't touch that, it's hot". She gave me an imperious look and said, "I like hot". A beautiful and funny moment and one that made me realise that she would be no pushover. Later in her life I was able to relate the story back to her and make the observation that she had a strong will and liked to discover and make up her own mind about things. This led to an intense discussion about her and the many facets of her identity.

It's a thousand small moments like this that give us insight into our children and help us and them build an understanding of who they are. Someone aptly said, "A woman doesn't want to be solved, she wants to be known". Recognising and calling out the identity of your child is one of the greatest gifts you can ever give them. It will set them on course for a meaningful and fulfilled life; a life of purpose. This is not only a gift to your child, it is a gift to the world.

You cannot help you child discover who they are if you don't spend a great deal of quality time with them and so the third dadverb is to **engage.** There is absolutely no substitute for in the moment, fully present time with your children. We impart the most important principles to our children while spending quality time with them, fully engaged with their hearts and minds. Trying to cram quality time into small gaps in a busy schedule seldom, if ever, works.

Author Spuds Crawford issued this profound challenge: "If something is truly important to you, then you should prove it. You say you would lay your life down for someone, but will you give them the busiest five minutes of your day, if they need it?"

This is relevant both to fathers living with their children and those who are not. The statistics for divorced fathers paint a very bleak picture. Research by the National Commission on Children *(Speaking of Kids,* 1991), found that ten years after the breakup of a marriage, more than two-thirds of kids report not having seen their father for a year. No matter how difficult, it is crucial that divorced fathers do whatever they can to spend regular, quality time with their children. "Live in" fathers too are often guilty of spending very little dedicated time with their children free of distractions.

For a number of years I ran an organisation called Outward Bound South Africa (OBSA). OBSA uses adventure and the outdoors to create learning experiences for people of all ages. Qualified instructors take participants on expeditions into the wilderness and expose them to a variety of obstacles and challenges. They then use these challenges to impart insights and life lessons to the participants. The challenges and experiences vary from one group to the next but the lessons they learn are profound and authentic.

Raising children is very similar. As fathers we need to spend time with our children, create different experiences for them and then use the opportunities that come up to impart wisdom and knowledge. It is a tough but sobering truth that you can see what a man values by what he spends his time and resources on. If you spend more time in front of the TV than engaging with your children then in reality you value TV time more than you value your children.

I remember one memorable experience with Luke when just the two of us went camping. After spending most of the day canoeing down a river we set up camp, lit a fire and sat under the stars talking for hours and hours. The conversation was enriching, filled with intriguing questions and animated discussion. So much richer and deeper than any conversation we would have had at home, immeasurably more meaningful and educational than sitting in front of TV together.

One December holiday Blythe and I took on the alphabet

DAD

challenge, doing one activity for each letter of the alphabet. For the letter A we invented an acting game, for B we played bat and ball on the beach, for C we went on an overnight camp, for D we went dancing, and so on. When we got to Z we couldn't find a zebra to ride so we ended up running madly across a zebra crossing. It turned out to be a lot more challenging than we thought but we managed to work our way through 26 activities. It created fun and joy, required imagination, action and effort but mostly it enabled us to spend great, quality time together and make beautiful memories.

It is important to dedicate time to spend exclusively with each of your children individually. This gives a powerful message to them that they matter, they are important and being with them is important to you as their father. One activity Blythe and I both loved was dancing lessons. Though our size differential made for some interesting variations to some tried and tested moves, we had wonderful times together.

An excellent practice is to take your children on dates. Let them decide where they want to go and just the two of you go and spend uninterrupted, fun time together doing what they love. At times the activities your children choose will be something you really enjoy doing, other times spending quality time with your child may mean doing things that really wouldn't be your first choice way to spend a few hours.

Blythe loves shopping. I really don't. Far more important than my dislike for shopping though is the fact that Blythe loves it and it has created a way for us to spend time together. I have spent countless hours scouring malls and waiting outside

CALL OUT

change rooms while Blythe tries on enough garments to outfit an entire fashion show. The lot of a man!

Spending quality time together creates great opportunities to impart wisdom and strength into your child's life. On one shopping expedition the mission was to buy a jacket for Blythe. As the day progressed and the number of jackets remaining to be tried on in the mall diminished to zero, I noticed Blythe getting quieter and quieter and more and more withdrawn. On the way home in the car, jacketless, I asked her what was wrong. She said that the jackets all made her look fat. What an opportunity to share with her how beautiful she is, how women throughout the world feel five kilograms bigger and dotted with cellulite every time they enter a brightly-lit changing room. By the time we got home Blythe was her normal happy self, and had gained important insight into life, self-esteem, the media and one more of the challenges of being a woman.

Some of the most profound interactions I have had with Luke have been during long road trips. For several years we would travel together every second weekend to the town in which Blythe lived with her mom. It was a five-hour journey each way and it provided an outstanding opportunity for deep, meaningful conversation about anything and everything. We still mention the rich and lively discussions we had on these trips.

Engaging with your children requires intent. If we are not careful, weeks can slip by without quality, meaningful time spent with them. It has been said that "being a great father is like shaving. No matter how well you shaved today, you have to do it again tomorrow". Remember that although your child may want material things, his or her deepest desire is to have you. And the less they have of you the more they will find other people and things to fill the void, some of which may be harmful to them.

Fun, quality, present, in the moment time with your child is an invaluable gift to your child and to yourself. At the end of your life you will never regret spending a little less time at the office but you will deeply regret not spending more time with your children. What you do with your time is the clearest illustration of what you truly value. Illustrate to your children and to the world that you value them.

By putting into practice the three dadverbs of seeing, identifying and engaging you will "call out" the identity of your children and help them discover who they are. Young men and women who have had a deeply involved father who called out their identity and allowed them to be fully who they are, have a rock solid foundation to build their lives on. A father who does this refuses to dictate a life script for his children but helps them to articulate the life story already written in their souls.

The true father sees what is already there. He calls to the man inside the boy and the woman inside the girl and says, "Come out, you have a role to play. Come out, you are good and worthy and the world needs what you have to offer. Come out and be fully you, fully alive".

Men and women who have experienced this from their fathers have no need to seek out their identity in illegitimate or harmful ways, joining gangs or groups who will lead them off track, obsessing with possessions and appearances, fads and fashions. They know who they are. Children who have been seen and known and cherished by their fathers have a secure foundation upon which to build a significant life. Fathers who get this right gift their children with a significant emotional advantage in life.

CHAPTER 5

Validate

"My father gave me the greatest gift anyone could give another person. He believed in me."
Jim Valvano.

The indispensable follow-on to calling out the identity of your child is to validate that identity. If the need to be seen is a universal cry then the need to be validated is its twin sister. So many people live their lives with a gnawing sense of illegitimacy, a sense that who they are is not enough. Every one of us needs to know that our life matters, that we count, that who we are is okay and good. And every one of us at some stage looked to our fathers to confirm and affirm this.

Fathers play a crucial role in establishing a young person's sense of validity and legitimacy. The fourth dadverb is to **affirm.** If we as fathers fail to do this, our children will look elsewhere for affirmation. When a girl hasn't heard from her father that she is lovely, nine times out of ten she will turn to another man to get the answer. When a boy hasn't heard from his father that he has what it takes to be a man, he will seek affirmation for his manhood in countless different ways, almost all harmful in some way or another.

DAD

How many times has the story played out where a woman is looking for love and finds a bogus form of it in the arms of a man seeking to affirm his masculinity through sexual conquest?

We as fathers need to let our children know that who they are is good, that their lives matter. Spending quality engaged time with them, as discussed in the previous chapter, lays a great foundation for affirmation as it shows in action not just word that they matter enough for us to dedicate our time, energy and resources to them. Words of affirmation build on this foundation. The words of a father have the power to build or to destroy. Authentic, truthful, thoughtful words of validation are powerful tools to build a child's sense of validity.

It is very important to be objective and genuine in affirming your child. There is a fine line between affirmation and flattery. Words of flattery generally cause more harm than good. Like eating candy floss, they feel good at the time but they have no real substance or value. They are sweet but empty. As a father it is very important to build integrity with your children by making sure that what you say is what you mean and that what you say is true and authentic.

There are two distinct categories of verbal affirmation. The first is affirming who your child is; that is a "being" affirmation. The second is affirming what your child does; that is a "doing" affirmation. Being affirmations are far more powerful than doing affirmations as they are not dependant on performance. Telling your children that they are wonderful for no other reason than you think they are wonderful has a profound impact on their sense of legitimacy and validity.

VALIDATE

If you only praise your child when he does something well, you are implicitly giving him the message that he is only worthwhile when he performs. Children need to know that you think they are great simply because they are who they are.

I used to sit Luke and Blythe on my lap individually when they were much younger and say in a number of different ways, "You are so wonderful". If they asked me why, I would respond, "Just because you are". They used to visibly swell. I felt an almost tangible force filling them with a profound assurance of their value and worth. I sometimes had to hide the emotion I felt, of seeing them so blessed and touched by my simple but heartfelt words.

Affirming your child for what they do is also very important. Success in life requires performing and as fathers we have to set standards for our children, encourage them to achieve and give honest feedback about their performance. There are many books written on this subject, but I will highlight some key points.

The first one is to be relevant and realistic in your expectations of your child. Relevant in that your expectations correspond to what your child wants and not just what you as a father want, and realistic in that they correspond to the level of skill and potential that your child actually has, not what you wish he had.

Knowing your child's likes and dislikes, strengths and weaknesses will help you to have relevant and realistic expectations of him or her. If you want your son to play rugby and he is built more like a piano player (I'm sure there are some powerfully built piano players out there, but work with me here), you will be doing your son great harm by expecting him to scrum down with his school's rugby team.

A good father will find out from his children what it is they want to do and then will spend time with them finding out their levels of talent and skill in that area. Based on these facts you will be able to help each child set relevant and realistic goals. No matter how competitive you are, remember that it is not only about winning. If your son or daughter loves doing something and they are not particularly talented at it, that's fine. It is far more important that they love what they do than that they compete at the highest level. As fathers we need to adjust our expectations to match our child's passions and potential.

One of the more challenging experiences I had with Luke was when he took up mixed martial arts quite seriously. This was very strange to me as Luke is a gentle and loving soul and the idea of him getting in a cage with another human being, both intent on beating each other half to death, just did not make sense to me. He loved it, however, so it was something I had to learn to validate him in.

At one of Luke's fights I remember sitting at the ringside with the father of one of Luke's friends who was also a fighter, and the two of us saying to each other that this was not what we'd signed up for. Why not synchronised swimming or table tennis? Luke turned out to be very good; he won the national under-18 championship in Jiu Jitsu and went on to represent South Africa internationally. For him it was a great self-esteem and character builder. For me it was a real stretch in accepting

VALIDATE

and affirming something that would not even have been on the list of activities I would have chosen for my son.

The most important thing to consider in praising our children for what they do is the attitude and character that they display in doing something. If we expect As on their report card and they are simply not A-level students, we need to make sure that we praise them when they do the best they can, even when they don't get top marks. Don't praise sub-par results when they stem from laziness or bad attitude, but do praise less than perfect results when you know that your child gave it his best shot.

Affirming your children is all about letting them know that they matter, that their lives counts and that you treasure and appreciate them. It's about letting them know that they are important and valuable. This leads to the fifth and probably most important dadverb of all, to **love.**

Children need to know above all else that they are loved and for love to be felt it must be expressed. Shakespeare said, "They do not love, that do not show their love." Every person has a unique way in which they want and need to receive love and as fathers we need to find out how best to express our love to each of our children.

Good dads love their children actively and generously and leave them in no doubt of their deep love and commitment to them. It's manly to be lavish in displaying your love and affection for your children. My view is that if your children occasionally find you a little over the top in your displays of affection for them, you are getting it right. If it comes from the right place they will forgive you.

I am unashamedly in love with Luke and Blythe. I tell them all the time and I show them constantly. When Blythe was a little younger I had love songs that I used to sing to her (very badly I might add!) and although she acted embarrassed at times, I know she liked it. One day one of the songs started playing on the radio and I was distracted and didn't sing along to her as I usually do. With a mixture of coyness and indignance, she said, "Hey dad, there's that song". She wanted me to sing it!

The message we as fathers give to our children must be clear: I love you with all my heart and I'm not ashamed to proclaim it in whatever way I can. That's the message that our sons and our daughters need to hear. Showing your daughter genuine love and deep affection throughout her childhood will teach her to expect that from the man she chooses later on and will protect her from accepting any less. Lavishing affection on your son will teach him to be at ease in receiving and expressing love and help him to be in touch with and comfortable with his own emotions.

One of the most important ways of expressing love is physical touch and affection. With Luke my displays of affection have generally taken a rough and tumble form, affectionate punching, wrestling and pushing, although there are times of hugging and holding. With Blythe there has been a lot of cuddling and hugging and walking arm in arm.

It is important to be aware of how your child wants to be shown affection. As Blythe has grown up the nature and tempo of our interaction and displays of affection have gone through different phases. As fathers we need to discern the slowly changing needs of our daughter's hearts and to match how we show our love to them. When Blythe was younger we would walk arm in arm through parks and malls, but now sometimes I notice that she needs a bit of distance between us as we walk, particularly when there are boys her age about.

Though the way I feel about her has not changed at all, I let her set the pace. As a young child Blythe loved showering with me and I used to wonder when the appropriate time would be for her to stop showering with her dad. I decided to completely leave it to her, to not make a fuss out of something she found so natural and fun. Slowly, as she approached puberty, she began to get a little more private until one day I realised she was no longer showering with me. There was no discussion, no issue, just a slow and very natural change.

Another very important way of expressing love for your children is simply telling them that you love them. From an early age, get into the habit of saying "I love you" to your children. This will teach them to freely express their feelings of love to you and it will help to create an environment of love and affection.

A crucial way of showing your children that you love them is by simply being available to them. Giving our children the highest position on our list of priorities tells them clearly that we love them. Constantly placing work, sporting and leisure activities above them shows them that we don't. There are many times that fathers need to put their children's needs above their own.

DAD

As a divorced man, this takes on a particular significance. At present I have the joy and privilege of having my sixteen-year-old daughter living under the same roof as me, but it was not always so. When we lived apart I phoned her every day, and I made sure that, unless it was really impossible, I always took her calls. There were times when I called her and I could sense that she was not in the mood to talk, while at other times it was impossible to get her to stop. The important thing was that I was continually and consistently reaching out to her, letting her know that I loved her, valued her and was available for her.

It's important to let our children set the pace in our communication with them; it's their hearts that are important here. The times when they want to speak at length are crucial; they need to know we are there for them, that nothing is more important than their hearts and that if they need to speak about anything, no matter how trivial, we as fathers are there for them.

Something you may notice as your child gets older is that it is easier to love a doting young child who has not yet formed his or her own opinion than a teenager who doesn't accept everything you say as gospel. The time comes when your child starts to develop strong ideas about life and begins talking back and questioning what you say. When this happens you as her father need to be solidly grounded in who you are and continue to show unconditional love. It is not about being right. What's important is not you and your ego, it is your child and her heart.

Affirming and loving our children leads to the sixth dadverb, which is to **bless**. Men and women who have received the blessing of their father have a quiet assurance about them. Women who have been blessed by their fathers know their worth and are unlikely to choose men who would neglect or abuse them. Men who have been blessed by their fathers know who they are and are free to pursue the life and career they desire, unaffected by the pressure of peers or popular culture.

The underlying message of the father's blessing is one of approval. It is an affirmation of who his child is, of his or her existence, validity and right to be alive and to prosper and have an impact in the world. This message can be given by a father to his child almost from conception: you are wanted, you were meant to be here, you count, I am glad you are alive, I am proud to be your father, I want you to be here, I want you to succeed, who you are and what you are destined for is important to me and to the world.

The father's blessing is imparted in countless different ways throughout his son and daughter's childhood, some of them tangible, some less obvious. It is through his words, his acts of love, his touch, his eyes, his body language. What is the feeling that your child gets from you in his or her day-to-day interaction with you? Are you a smiling, caring, approving man? Or are you disapproving or preoccupied? The way you are with your child in general day-to-day living imparts or withholds blessing. Be a loving, approving, accepting father who creates an atmosphere of positivity and possibility for your children.

Another key way of imparting your blessing as a father is through thoughtful celebration of key milestones in your children's lives. A 13th birthday is significant, as is a 16th,

18th and 21st. Each of these important birthdays presents an opportunity for a father to impart his blessing. Thoughtful, symbolic gifts and carefully chosen words can impart a strong message of validation and approval.

One of the tragedies of our modern culture is a lack of tradition and rituals that provide opportunities to impart blessing to our children. Because of this, for Luke's 13th birthday I decided to create a rites of passage ritual for him. I invited eight men who possessed integrity and qualities I wanted to see passed on to Luke. I asked each of them to prepare a short message for Luke about what it means to be a man and to buy a gift that represented the message they wanted to impart.

My gifts to Luke were a sword, a compass and a crystal with a cross and the words 'nothing is impossible' engraved into it. The compass represented Luke's moral core, his true north, the values and principles that would guide him through the rest of his life, and I committed myself to teach him and help him discover for himself what these values are. The crystal represented his potential. I talked about the power that is contained in one atom and that in Luke was the potential to significantly influence the world.

I told him that as his father I believed in him and would do everything I could to help him discover and realise his full potential. The sword represented battle. I told Luke that not everything would come easily and I gave him permission to fight for what he believed and I committed to doing all I could to equip him for the battle.

It was a profoundly moving experience for all of us. I had

the privilege of blessing my son in the presence of a group of men who added weight to my blessing with their words and presence. I have subsequently had the honour of conducting a number of such rituals for young men and each time it has had a profound effect on all involved.

I went away recently with a group of seven other men on an informal retreat. Part of the process was an agreement to speak openly into each other's lives as fellow men. As the weekend progressed, it became clear that several of the men had grown up without having fully received their father's blessing. We put together a ceremony on the Sunday morning in which we called these men out and acknowledged and blessed them as men. The effect was astounding.

Each man who went through the process was deeply and profoundly touched. There was not a dry eye as one by one we went through the process of being seen and acknowledged and blessed by fellow men. It highlighted to us all just how much a father's blessing is needed and just how little it is given.

Boys and girls alike need to receive their father's blessing. A father's blessing is his emotional, physical and spiritual embrace. It's an embrace that's there even when the father is not, lingering in his absence to validate, comfort and guide. A man or woman who has truly experienced their father's blessing will wear it for the rest of their life; a cloak of assurance wrapped around their soul that fits no-one else but them.

Validating our children means raising them in such a way that when they reach adulthood they have a rich storehouse in their souls of their father's affirmation, love and blessing expressed innumerable times and in innumerable ways. They have a sure sense of their worth; they are in no doubt whatsoever that the man who fathered them approves of who they are as a unique human being. This is a gift they will never lose and that no-one can ever steal from them.

CHAPTER 6

Create a Sanctuary

"Our own front door can be a wonderful thing, or a sight we dread; rarely is it only a door."
Jeanette Winterson

The environment in which our children grow up plays a crucial role in determining whether they thrive or merely survive. And as fathers we play a primary role in creating this environment. American educator and author Reed Markham said it plainly: "Every father is the architect of his home life." Strong, loving, present dads create an atmosphere of warmth, safety and joy in which their children flourish. Angry, abusive fathers create a fearful atmosphere laced with dread in which their children retreat into themselves and their rooms. Absent dads leave a sad vacuum in which their children are forced to find their way without his wisdom and strength.

As fathers we have the ability and the responsibility to create an environment which will nourish and protect our sons and daughters and enable them to thrive. The environment that we create has physical, emotional and spiritual elements, all of which are vitally important. Just as a gardener tends to his nursery to make sure that the conditions are ideally suited to each tree that he plants, so we as fathers need to tend to the environment in which our children live.

Taking the gardening metaphor further, every seed of a particular species of tree that is planted has the same innate potential but the extent to which each one reaches this potential is determined by the conditions in which it grows. The soil in which it is planted, the water and nourishment it receives, the amount of sunlight it gets and the extent to which it is protected from extreme elements determines how much of its potential will unfold. Trees growing in a poor environment may be resilient (if they survive), but they will also be stunted and fall short of their intended height and strength. As fathers it is our responsibility to create an environment in which our children will grow to their full potential.

The first dadverb in creating a sanctuary for our children is to **nurture**. Although women are natural and gifted nurturers it is not their exclusive domain, nor their job to perform alone. Men are not only capable of nurturing their children but have a duty to do so. Children need to be nurtured by their fathers. Through nurture our children learn that masculine strength is safe and gentle, that power can be used tenderly to hold and comfort and assure.

One of the most important things a man can do to create a nurturing environment for his children is to love, affirm, protect and honour their mother. A woman who is loved by the father of her children is empowered to give her nurturing best, and a mom's nurture is of incalculable value to her children. A wise dad knows this and gives to the mother of his children the

CREATE A SANCTUARY

love and protection she needs to be her best.

It is both natural and manly for a man to nurture his children. Nurture is showing the softer, gentler side of yourself to your children. It is showing understanding when they are hurt or down or discouraged. It is holding them gently, speaking kind words, having them sit on your lap, letting them fall asleep in your arms.

When Blythe was younger I used to sit on the side of her bed and stroke her hair as she drifted off to sleep. I would stop only when I heard the deep, even breathing of sleep. If I stopped a moment too soon she would murmur for me to continue. These were precious times of nurture. She felt safe in my presence, my physical touch was calming and re-assuring and there was a transfer of affection and strength to her. Even to this day if she is struggling to sleep or feeling anxious about something I sit on her bed and gently stroke her hair as she drifts off to sleep. It's truly beautiful; a young woman safe in her father's embrace, a treasured time of togetherness, a special gift to me and to her.

A father's nurture is felt in his consistent, steady presence. It's evident in his kind look, his loving touch, his gentle voice, his tender tone. A father's nurture is physical, emotional, and spiritual. It is touch, words, prayer. A father's nurture gives, never takes. It imparts life. It creates a space where a child feels free to be exactly who he or she is. A space where a boy or girl feels safe, loved, wanted; a place where their hearts find both solace and expression.

Key to nurturing your child is to respect them. By respecting your child you teach them that they matter, that their time, their space, their possessions, what they say and do is valuable. Showing them respect is as simple as knocking on their door before walking in, asking permission to use their things, and listening to what they say. It's as simple as respecting what they do and don't like, giving credibility to their opinion and validity to their feelings.

A child who has been nurtured this way has a deep sense of safety and value. He or she understands intimacy, is equipped to nurture others and will trust easily. This makes the next dadverb particularly important and that is to **protect.** Sigmund Freud said "I cannot think of any need in childhood as strong as the need for a father's protection".

The instinct to protect from harm lies at the core of a man's masculinity, and it is an immensely powerful force. One of the primary duties of a father is to create a safe physical and emotional environment for his children. In order for our children to flourish they need to know that they are safe. Many animal species simply stop producing when the environment becomes dangerous.

The job of protecting our children has become harder and more complex over the years. In some ways it must have been easier when the most dangerous enemy was a sabre-tooth tiger. You knew what the enemy was and you knew how to fight it off; a few arrows and some spear-throwing practice and you were ready for that cat!

Much has changed. Now the dangers that our children face are a lot more subtle and numerous. And they are no longer

CREATE A SANCTUARY

all "out there". Many are beamed into the sanctity of our own homes via TV and the Internet. Too many children today have almost constant unsupervised access to Internet, television and social networking, which can expose them to some pretty nasty stuff.

The way in which men treat women has changed too. Respect for women seems to have reached an all-time low. Just how far gone the days of chivalry are was revealed to me in a recent incident. Blythe and two of her friends were seated at the back of a school bus waiting for it to leave when a young man, a year older than them, approached them and demanded in a rude and aggressive way that they move as they were in his seat. Being the assertive young lady that she is, Blythe refused, rightly stating that everyone was free to sit wherever they wanted. The boy became agitated and started swearing at them until they felt threatened and decided to move.

It was not too long ago that young men would get up off their seats and offer them to young ladies. It was the polite and accepted thing to do. Somehow in the space of a few decades the way men treat women has degenerated from polite and respectful to aggressive and disrespectful. Our daughters need protecting and our sons need educating!

Being a father to a girl brings its own unique challenges. The spectre of boyfriends looms ever closer on the horizon and the day inevitably comes when, like a pack of wolves, they start circling around your daughter's door. Dealing with the boys that will inevitably come into your daughter's life is a challenge for most doting dads.

DAD

It's very important that all prospective boyfriends are fully aware that if they do anything to hurt your precious girl it could well be the last thing they ever do. But it's also important for them to like you and to want to hang out with you. It's an artful balancing act between being welcoming and at the same time threatening. If they consider you cool but dangerous you've got it just right.

Once a friend of Luke's hugged Blythe for longer than the requisite nano-second and I felt deeply primal feelings stirring within me. As this lecherous young man, positively reeking with impure thoughts, clung lasciviously to my daughter, the desire to remove his head from his shoulders with my bare hands all but overwhelmed me. I realised that perhaps I was being slightly irrational and that it was after all a simple hug, so I kept my feelings to myself and he went on his way blissfully unaware of the near death experience he had just had.

Humour aside, your daughter needs to know that her father is there to fight for her in any way she may need. This knowledge fills young girls with a sense of worth and safety. This is the dad's role and it can only be properly fulfilled if you are there, if you know who her friends are, who she hangs out with, who she likes. It means being closely and actively involved. If she knows that she is worth fighting for she will not accept any man in her life that is not willing to give his all to protect her.

Protecting our children involves four key elements, the first of which is awareness. As fathers we need to make it our business to know what our children are exposed to in every aspect of their lives, the friends they hang out with, their

CREATE A SANCTUARY

school environment, the places they go to, the programmes they watch, the social media they engage with. Being aware enables you to take appropriate action to protect your child from potential danger.

I am constantly amazed by how many parents allow their children to sleep over at a friend's house whose parents they have never even spoken to, let alone met. If Blythe wants to go to a friend's house for a party or dinner or sleep over, I make sure that I meet the parents, get a good sense of the kind of people they are, establish what the curfew is, if there will be adults around, get their telephone numbers and find out what the plans are.

Blythe sometimes finds this a little embarrassing and rolls her eyes when I get out of the car to meet the parents, but she also appreciates it. She feels valued and protected. I let her know that I trust her fully but that I don't want her to ever be in a situation where she feels threatened or compromised. As fathers we need to know where our children are, who they are friends with, what they watch and listen to. We cannot be with them at all times but we can develop eyes and ears to know what is happening in their lives.

The second key element to protecting our children is education. As adults we have been around longer than our children and we know a few things they don't. As men we know how boys think; it wasn't too long ago that we were one of them. We know the dangers of the Internet, of media, of social networking (and if we don't, we need to learn). We need to take time to teach our children about what is out there and equip them to deal with it. Because we cannot be with them 24 hours a day, we must equip them to deal with any unsavoury situation they may have to face without us.

When Blythe turned 13 I had a long discussion with her about passing from being a girl to becoming a woman. We developed a lexicon of words and terms to help define this passage. One of the words we used to describe this time was "wogirl". It meant halfway between being a woman and being a girl. It also played on the expression "whoa girl". Wait. There is no hurry to get involved in certain activities reserved for later in life

It was a beautiful discussion about life, womanhood, boys, sex, drugs, dangers, joys, pleasures, boundaries and the plethora of challenges and delights that awaited her. We used the analogy of an enchanted forest that she was walking through into womanhood and all the challenges and joys she would face and how to deal with them. I said to her that my role is like Merlin the wizard, there whenever she called on me to offer wisdom, whatever magic I could conjure, and to fight for her with every fibre of my being.

In spite of how difficult or awkward it may be, we need to keep our children informed about life and the challenges it presents. After the divorce, Blythe moved in with her new step family of three brothers and a step-father. Given that the prevalence of sexual abuse is much higher in step families, I felt the need to have a conversation with her about this. Simply discussing such an awful topic with an innocent 11-year-old beauty felt like a violation but it was necessary to let her know

CREATE A SANCTUARY

about the real world and the dangers it holds.

In that specific instance it turned out to be unnecessary as the family she moved in with were a wholesome crew, but I made sure she was prepared. As fathers we need to keep our sons and daughters appropriately informed of the realities and dangers of life.

The third element of protecting our children is presence. Nothing is more important in a father's lexicon as the two words "be there". When you are present and engaged in your children's lives you will quickly discern when all is not well. You will know them and develop a sense of what is going on inside them. If you are available and accessible your child will feel free to share with you anything that may be concerning or upsetting him or her. This presence and availability will enable you to deal with issues or situations that may become harmful to your child quickly, before they become more serious.

Finally we need to be willing and ready to fight for our children. Our children must know that they have a man in their corner, their father. And they and everyone who knows them must know that that man will stand up and fight for them if anything or anyone threatens them. You may need to confront a bully, or a teacher or headmaster, or involve yourself in an incident which took place that upset them. Your children need to know that you are willing to put yourself on the line for them, to stand up and fight for them.

One of the key things that a man has to protect his family from is lack and that leads to the ninth dadverb, to **provide.**

In our highly materialistic world the pressure to provide

the right size house in the right neighbourhood with the right car and all the right accessories can be overwhelming. But providing for your children does not mean keeping up with the proverbial Joneses. What is important is that you provide to the best of your abilities a good home, a solid education and as much financial security as you are able. Never forget that what your children need most of all is a present and engaged father.

If in your quest to provide bigger, better and cooler you find yourself with less and less time for your family, your priorities have slipped and you need to reassess. Your children need to live safely, comfortably, receive a good education and have their parents with them in a happy home. That is all. Anything other than this is nice to have but not essential. The poorest dad can leave behind the richest inheritance because it takes very little money to give what's most important to your child.

The two extremes that men often go to are either to pursue wealth and success at the expense of being there for their family or to abandon them and look for any excuse not to assist financially. It goes without saying that both are damaging and unacceptable and to be avoided at all costs.

Providing for children can come at a great personal sacrifice, especially for divorced dads, who often find themselves having to fund their own home and living expenses as well as contributing substantially to the home and living expenses of their ex-wife. However onerous it may be, providing for your children is a non-negotiable obligation for a father. If you can provide you must provide. It's as simple as that. If it requires a drop in living standards so that your children can be taken care

CREATE A SANCTUARY

of, so be it. A real man never walks away from his responsibility to provide for his children.

The two obvious keys to providing for your children are earning money and prioritising expenses. The first simply means being industrious and applying yourself to working hard and smart to earn sufficient income to support your family and provide for your and their future. The second means living within your means and placing the needs of your children at the top of your priority list. It may mean holding on to that car for a few years longer before upgrading so that you can afford to pay for a good school, or forgoing that flat screen television so that you can pay for your daughter's horse riding lessons.

By nurturing, protecting and providing we create a sanctuary in which our children can flourish and grow to their full potential. It is our joy and responsibility as fathers to work hard to create this safe and enabling environment. It is in the safety of this sanctuary we are best able to equip our children for life, which is the topic of the next chapter.

CHAPTER 7

Equip for Life

"The aim of education is to develop resources in the child that will contribute to his well-being as long as life endures; to develop power of self-mastery that he may never be a slave to indulgence or other weaknesses, to develop [strong] manhood, beautiful womanhood to face life with courage, meet disaster with fortitude, and face death without fear."
David O. McKay

The ultimate goal of parenthood is to equip your children so that they don't need you. The ultimate reward of parenthood, if you get it right, is that your children will always want you. As fathers we are there for our children; they are not there for us. As an involved father you will receive immeasurable joy and fulfilment from fathering your children, but your primary role is to give to them, not receive from them.

Our lives as men are ours to live. Any mistakes we may have made are our own, any lost opportunities were our own missed chances, any regrets are ours to deal with. The children we now father have their own lives to live and it is our role as fathers to equip them to live their lives to the full. And to do so we need to put aside any expectations we have for them which come from our own unresolved issues and focus on them and their unique destinies.

Author Helen Romos made the profound statement that one father is more than a hundred schoolmasters. The 10th dadverb is to **teach.** During the course of their childhood your children will benefit from many teachers and educators but you as their father are the most important teacher they will ever have. You are the one who is most instrumental in equipping your children with the skills they need to succeed.

This is not to say that you know more than their teachers or are more skilled than their coaches. Gifted teachers and coaches play an invaluable role in teaching our children the things we cannot, but in their school of life we play the role of principal. We are the conductor of their education orchestra. We ensure that our children get exposed to the right learning experiences and environments. We make sure that what they are passionate about they have an opportunity to learn and experience.

There are two types of education every child needs: formal and informal. Formal education in many ways is the easier of the two. It is primarily outsourced to schools, colleges and other learning institutions. A father's role in providing a formal education for his children is simply to get them into the best educational institutions he can afford and provide them with the support and encouragement to do their best in them.

The informal aspect of our children's education is a lot more complicated. It involves teaching them the life skills they will need to make a success of their lives. For the most part, this teaching cannot be outsourced. In many ways, life skills

EQUIP FOR LIFE

are more important than formal education. If someone has good life skills but insufficient formal education they will have a good chance of succeeding in life, even educating themselves further if needed. If someone has a good formal education but very poor life skills, chances are they will make a mess of their life.

The concept "life skills" covers a broad range of emotional, mental, physical and spiritual skills that equip a person to succeed in all aspects of their life. The first and possibly most important of these is Emotional Intelligence or EQ. In a nutshell, EQ is the ability to manage yourself and your emotions well and to interact authentically and successfully with others. It is the health of your relationship with yourself and with others.

A person with a high EQ knows and understands himself and can control his feelings, thoughts and actions well. He is mature and is able to interact skilfully with others and build harmonious and mutually beneficial relationships. For a graphic illustration of people who have dangerously low EQ, watch an episode of Jerry Springer! People with low EQ are unable to handle their own feelings, urges and selfish desires. Their lives are about themselves and their own personal gratification. They are also very poor at relationships, spending a lot of time and energy in conflict with those around them.

The ability to be in touch with their feelings and to deal appropriately with them is one of the most fundamental life skills we need to teach our children. Emotions are natural and good and if understood and managed are one of the greatest gifts we have. Some emotions are much easier to deal with than others. Joy is a beautiful emotion that is easy to handle. Anger, on the other hand, is more difficult to deal with. There are a few key steps in helping your children deal with their emotions.

The first is to identify the emotion. Children often don't have the ability to put their feelings into words and we as their fathers need to help them develop an emotional vocabulary. (To be honest, the emotional vocabulary of men can also be somewhat limited!) Children need to be able to identify and acknowledge what they are feeling and put words to it.

The second step is to validate the emotion. No emotion is wrong in and of itself. Every emotion we or our children feel is valid and okay. What's important is how they deal with it. It's okay to be angry, but it's not okay to hit the person who made you angry. It's fine to feel sad, but it's not fine to allow that to develop into depression. Emotions are our heart's way of telling us what's going on inside us. They are healthy and good.

The third step is to find the source of the emotion; to identify its cause. Often teenagers will feel a general sense of emotional malaise but when questioned are unable to articulate why. As fathers we need to help our children to understand why they are feeling the emotions they are. Once the reason for the feeling has been established it is much easier to deal with it.

The final step is to teach your children how to deal appropriately with their emotion. This presents a great opportunity to teach them a wide range of life skills. If your son comes home sullen and angry and after some probing you discover that he feels unfairly treated by one of his teachers, grab this opportunity with both hands. If he is feeling angry and resentful you will need to teach him the need to forgive and let go. If he is feeling upset with himself for under-performing, you can teach him about forgiving himself and self-acceptance. If there is an element of fear you can teach him how to face up to his fears and overcome them. If there is an element of unfairness you can teach him to be assertive and deal with the person behind the problem, even modelling the way for him by going with him to see the offending individual.

When Luke first moved in with me after his mother and I were divorced there was a range of emotions brewing within him. It took hours of conversation over weeks and months to help him understand what he was feeling, to let him know that what he was feeling was normal and okay, to identify why he was feeling what he was and to assist him to deal with these feelings in a wise and appropriate way.

One of the feelings he had to deal with was anger towards his parents for divorcing. It is very difficult for a young child to acknowledge that they are angry with the parents they love and want to please. Often the anger plays itself out in rebellious or self-destructive behaviour, which neither parent nor child fully understands. By following the four steps it is possible to completely defuse negative emotions and turn them into a powerful learning and growing experience.

I had the privilege of helping Luke identify the fact that he was feeling angry and that the anger was with me and his mom. I was able to validate this emotion and let him know it was fine for him to feel the way he did. I let him know that the divorce wasn't his fault, that it was our fault as his parents. I was able to help him deal with it through forgiveness and understanding and embracing the new reality of his life.

This and many other emotions we dealt with following the four steps. I cannot begin to say what an empowering experience this was for both of us. What could have been a destructive experience resulting in an angry, rebellious teenager turned into a powerful learning experience. Going through this experience accelerated the development of Luke's EQ and equipped him with crucial life skills to manage both himself and others

Another invaluable life skill we need to teach our children is personal accountability. It is in our nature to blame others for the things that go wrong in our lives. One of the marks of successful people is that they take personal responsibility for all that happens in their life. As fathers we need to clearly teach our children that everything they do has a consequence and that they need to take full responsibility for the consequences of their actions.

Once again we need to lead by example. If you are continually complaining about the economy, the government, the price of petrol and so on, and blaming your circumstances on things over which you have no control, you cannot expect your child to learn how to take responsibility for his own life.

One of the fascinating and sometimes amusing interplays in my relationship with Luke and Blythe has been how they look after their possessions. When things would get broken or lost their immediate response was to say, "Dad, it's not my fault". The excuses were numerous: "I lent it to Fred and he broke it",

"I left it next to my locker and it went missing", "I slipped and it fell out of my hands". It took a long time for them to grasp that no matter what the reason for the loss or breakage, if it was in their care at the time it was their responsibility and they had to deal with the consequences.

This lesson of cause and effect, of action and consequence is key to your child's success in life. People who take responsibility for their actions have a far greater chance of succeeding and being happy in life. And it is a key lesson that we as fathers need to teach and to model.

Closely related to this is cultivating an attitude of gratitude. Teaching your child to be grateful and thankful for all that is good in their lives will develop an attitude that will endear them to people and go a long way towards ensuring their happiness. Thankful people are happy people. Ungrateful, complaining people are by definition never happy with what they have and are therefore generally miserable.

Finally, one of the greatest life skills you can teach your child is the power of a habit. Simple daily habits in all the important areas of one's live build a great life. A mere 20 minutes a day of reading translates to 140 minutes a week, close to 10 hours a month and over 120 hours a year, which is 15 full working days! That's a lot of reading achieved by a simple, daily, 20-minute habit. I remember as a young man going away on holiday with a friend and we got into the habit of doing some sit ups every morning. It took less than 10 minutes a day and it was amazing what a difference it made to the strength and tone of our stomachs over the course of a few short weeks.

In every area of life, physical, spiritual, emotional, relational, mental, financial, there are good habits that you can help your child develop. Do this and you will equip them for life. The power of good habits is enormous; so, unfortunately, is the power of bad habits. As the well-known saying goes, "Sow an act, and you reap a habit; sow a habit, and you reap a character; sow a character, and you reap a destiny". Great lives are built on simple acts done repeatedly over a lifetime.

Teaching your child to practise good habits leads to the 11th dadverb, which is **discipline.** As a father you are not in a popularity contest with your children on the panel of judges, neither are you your children's friend. You are their father and there will be times when you will need to make some hard calls. You cannot be a good father if you are concerned more with your children's approval than with what is good for them. Author Victor Devlin puts it plainly when he writes, "Listen, there is no way any true man is going to let children live around him in his home and not discipline and teach, fight and mould them until they know all he knows. His goal is to make them better than he is. Being their friend is a distant second to this."

A good father doesn't just affirm his children but lovingly disciplines them too. Affirmation without discipline is the beginning of delusion. Well known philosopher Goethe rightly said, "Too many parents make life hard for their children by trying, too zealously, to make it easy for them." Discipline is a vitally important part of equipping children for life. It starts with setting boundaries for our children's behaviour. Boundaries are clear guidelines about what is acceptable and what is not. Children need to have clear and consistent behavioural boundaries in which they know they can operate freely. Not only does this teach them right from wrong, it provides them with a sense of emotional security.

In order to set and maintain clear boundaries, the authority you have in your children's lives needs to be effective and legitimate. Your response to this statement may well be, "I'm their dad and they must listen to me!" While your position as father carries some measure of authority, it is not enough. To maintain legitimate authority and influence you need to build on the positional authority you have as your children's father by developing personal authority.

Positional authority comes by simply being a father; personal authority is earned by fathering. The older your child becomes the less you can rely on positional authority and the more you need to rely on the personal power you have earned over the course of his childhood. Dads who rely purely on their position as father or on physical strength and fear to get their children to comply, have lost a crucial battle in boundary setting.

Personal power is the level of credibility you have with and influence you have over your children. It comes as a result of the way that you father them and lead your own life and it is built on four pillars. The first of these is love. If your children know without a shadow of doubt that you love them, because you have shown them both in word and in deed, they are likely to accept the boundaries you set a whole lot more readily. The beautiful guarantee of love is that a child who is truly loved will always desire the approval of the one who truly loves him and a father who truly loves will always desire the very best for the child he loves.

The second pillar of personal power is integrity. This means matching your actions to your words and doing what you say. You simply will not have credibility with your children if you don't practise what you preach. If you say one thing and do another, or expect your children to live a certain way while you live another, you might as well let them do as they please because they certainly won't want to do what you say.

If your children know that when you say something you mean it and it will not change no matter what, your words will carry so much more weight. If you tell your child that you will send him to his room if he doesn't stop whining and he doesn't, you must follow through on the threat. If you don't, you have effectively lied to your child and he will take you less seriously. The other great benefit of practising this level of integrity is that it forces you to think carefully before you say anything. It builds credibility and adds weight to your words.

The third pillar is consistency. It is crucial that the boundaries you set as a father don't change from day to day depending on your mood and availability. It is also crucial that you don't allow your children to manipulate and wear you down. Your yes must be yes and your no, no. If your children know that they can change your mind or the rules if they just ask you enough times, your word becomes negotiable and you will lose credibility and authority.

The final and perhaps most challenging pillar of personal power is wisdom. You need to carefully and prayerfully consider

EQUIP FOR LIFE

the boundaries you set for your children, research what the experts say, study scripture for Godly principles, discuss with your wife to benefit from her wisdom. We need to ensure that what we ask of our children is wise and good.

Remember that you cannot and must not always reason with a young child. There will be times when they just don't get it and when an explanation doesn't work because they are simply too young to understand. Fathers who treat their children as mini adults are setting the stage for a lot of heartache. Young children are not mini adults and they do not yet have the wisdom to guide their actions. That is what you their dad are there for, to impart wisdom and understanding over time. Allowing your children to do what they want and get away with violating the boundaries you set spoils them. They will likely grow up undisciplined and disrespectful.

A truly remarkable illustration of discipline and boundary setting came from events that unfolded at Pilansberg, the fourth largest game reserve in South Africa. Several young elephants who had been orphaned in a culling operation some years before started displaying disturbingly destructive behaviour. As they started maturing these young elephants began attacking and killing rhinos – behaviour not seen before by wild life experts. In an attempt to curb this abnormal behaviour a few mature bull elephants were brought into the park. Almost immediately the young bulls stopped attacking rhino and started behaving normally. The older bull elephants quickly restored proper boundaries to their behaviour. What a wonderful illustration from the animal kingdom of the importance of older males setting boundaries for younger males and keeping their behaviour in check.

As you discipline your children you will be teaching them to discipline themselves. Author Jim Rohn so wisely said, "We must all suffer one of two things: the pain of discipline or the pain of regret or disappointment". Discipline is the bridge between goals and accomplishment and therefore vital to success. Without self-discipline nothing great is ever achieved. We give our children an invaluable gift by teaching them to delay gratification and do the difficult things first. The ability to say no to oneself builds success and creates a sense of dignity.

Author and biologist Thomas Huxley said, "Perhaps the most valuable result of all education is the ability to make yourself do the thing you have to do, whether you like it or not." Discipline is a compulsory subject in the life education we as fathers need to give our children. Irish Philosopher Edmund Burke said, "It is ordained in the eternal constitution of things, that men of intemperate minds cannot be free. Their passions forge their fetters." For our children to lead free, whole and successful lives, we must teach them discipline.

A good father will not be afraid to set and defend clear boundaries. You will find yourself defending your children's boundary lines from both sides. They will push the boundaries from the inside out and the world will push them from the outside in. Maintaining healthy boundaries is the role of father as protector and discipliner.

The twelfth and final dadverb is to **model.** As discussed in chapter three, how you live your life speaks louder and more clearly to your children than anything you say to them. Who you are as a father is far more important to your children than what you have, and of far greater consequence and impact than the words you speak.

For fathers to truly have an impact on the way our children grow up, we need to live what we teach our kids. It is of no value to teach your child about fitness and good dietary habits if you are a couch potato, constantly shovelling junk food into your mouth. Your words will be meaningless and you will come across as a fat hypocrite, literally!

The old adage, "Do as I say and not as I do" must be treated with contempt by any real father. Your life is your primary message to your children. Live it well and chances are, they will too. Live it badly and chances are, well, they will too. The question every father needs to ask himself is, "Am I truly the kind of man I would like my son to become or my daughter to marry one day? Inside and out, am I really that man?" If we can't answer "yes" then we must at least be able to say, "I may not be yet, but I am working hard on becoming that man."

It is a sad reality that so many men are trying not to be like their fathers and so many women end up with men who are wrong for them because they are still trying to fix what was dysfunctional in their fathers. As fathers we must make every effort to be the kind of man who inspires our sons to want to be like us, and who sets the standard for the kind of man our daughters will marry one day.

To maximise the positive impact we have on our children and truly equip them for life, our lives must be an attractive example of all that we want them to become. Fatherhood demands authenticity (and there is no greater test of authenticity than a teenager). Your greatest parenting tool is the life you live. If there is any discrepancy between what you say to your son or daughter and how you live your life, what you are trying to impart will be completely lost. Your actions must be consistent with your words.

As a divorced man, for instance, it is important to put away any anger or hostility towards your ex-wife and show your children grace and forgiveness in action. If you carry bitterness and anger it will poison you and affect the way you behave towards her. Whether you say anything or not, your children will discern this and in effect you will be teaching them to harbour resentment, to be bitter, and to not forgive.

If you are a man of faith then your life must reflect that and reveal qualities in action that your children respect and desire and will ultimately seek to emulate. If your children look at the life you live and it is desirable to them, they are likely to want to adopt your beliefs and values. If they see you miserable and judgemental, they will most certainly challenge and probably walk away from your belief system.

If you want your children to respect you, respect them; if you want them to eat well and lead active lives, then eat well and lead an active life. If you want your children to read the right books and watch the right movies, read them and watch them yourself. There is no guarantee that your children will pick up all of your good habits as they are individuals who will ultimately need to choose their own way. There is a firm guarantee, however, that if your life does not match up to your words you will lose their respect and your words will be meaningless to them. The greater the discrepancy between your life and your words, the quicker you will move from being important in their lives to being impotent.

This is challenging stuff. But what greater motivation can we have as men than the knowledge that the way we live our lives will profoundly influence the way our children turn out? If we love them enough we simply have to get our act together. The joy and rewards of putting into practise the 12 dadverbs are immeasurable and the impact will resound through multiple generations.

PART THREE

THE CHALLENGE

CHAPTER 8

Man in the Mirror

"A man should be able to hear, and to bear, the worst that could be said of him."
Saul Bellow

The last section of this book is called "The Challenge" because that is what it is. It contains a series of practical exercises to help you put into practice the principles presented in the first two sections.

To recap some of the key points:

1. A father's impact on his children is powerful and profound and lasts throughout their lives; that's a given. Whether this impact is positive or negative is each father's choice.
2. True masculinity is at the core of true fatherhood.
3. To be great fathers we need to deal with our own inner wounds and live with authentic masculinity.
4. The title "father" is not something we attain through the birth of our child but something we earn by

countless acts of fathering.
5. The way we live speaks louder to our children than anything we say to them.
6. We can only impart to our children what we have inside us to give.
7. What we have inside us, both good and bad, will be imparted in some degree to our children.
8. The parallel journey of fatherhood means we need to learn to be and become a man as we nurture and teach our sons to become men and our daughters to become women.

To be great fathers we need to work both on the way we live and our inner lives. This is a process of personal transformation and the starting point of transformation is to look in the mirror.

Men are notoriously bad at asking for directions because we don't like to show any weakness. It threatens our manliness. We would sooner drive around for hours, bearing the scorn and wrath of our wives and partners, before admitting that we need help. The same applies to our lives. We hate to admit that our lives may not be all they were intended to be, and we hate asking for help.

But every one of us has blind spots, aspects of our lives that need growth and development and change. And just as we rely on mirrors to see our reflection in order to shave, so we need mirrors that reflect back to us our behaviour as men and the impact this has on other people. The best mirrors are the people who know us well: our families, friends and work colleagues. And often the most effective mirrors are the people who rub us up the wrong way. People who really push our buttons are a gift as they reveal to us what we need to work on in ourselves.

The exercises that follow provide an opportunity to take an honest look at yourself as a man and father. As you go through them, resolve to be brutally honest with yourself. Keep in mind what author and activist Gloria Steinem said: "The truth will set you free, but first it will piss you off."

The areas that need the most growth are probably those that you see least clearly and will need the help of others to see. Friends, colleagues and family members are invaluable in assisting you on this journey. Ask your wife and children for their feedback; ask parents, siblings, colleagues. Become conscious and commit to growing as a man and becoming a great father. It is not an overnight process; personal transformation takes time, effort and commitment. Most of all it takes a willingness to embrace the truth.

Before starting this process ask yourself the question, "am I willing to look honestly at myself as a man and as a father, accept whatever blind spots I may have and make whatever changes may be necessary?" If your answer is "yes" then let's get going! This could change your life and your children's lives forever.

Take some time to reflect on the questions that are posed in the next two chapters. Set aside time to think deeply before you answer. Write down your answers in a personal journal or on a piece of paper that you can throw away once you are finished. This is for your eyes only. This is not the kind of process that can be squeezed into a spare 10 minutes whenever the mood hits. It needs dedicated open-ended time, but is well worth whatever time you give to it.

Challenge One: The dadquizz

Rate yourself as a father by filling in the following dadquizz. For each statement give yourself a score between 1 and 10. Then ask your wife and your children to do the same for you, without showing them your scores. If you are not married to your child's mother, make sure she fills this out too. You may not like or agree with her input but be open to it. The more honest you are with yourself and the freer your family feels to be honest with you, the more effective this exercise will be. See this as a starting point for your growth as a father.

1. I know my child's heart, their likes and dislikes, fears and dreams. I know what makes them come alive and what makes them sad. I know because I truly listen to my children and empathise with their feelings.

    My score: _____ *Mother's score:* _____ *Child's score:* _____

2. I know my children's unique talents, abilities and personality traits. I value them above my own expectations and do all I can to develop them as unique individuals so that they discover their purpose and excel in life.

   My score: _____ Mother's score: _____ Child's score: _____

3. I regularly spend dedicated quality time individually with each of my children. I make sure that we do what they enjoy and that I am present and engaged, free from distractions.

   My score: _____ Mother's score: _____ Child's score: _____

4. I consciously and consistently validate and affirm my children with words and I back this up with my body language.

   My score: _____ Mother's score: _____ Child's score: _____

5. My children know without any doubt that I love them. I express my love to them by telling them with my words and showing them consistently and regularly with my actions.

   My score: _____ Mother's score: _____ Child's score: _____

DAD

6. My children know that they have my approval, that I want them and cherish them.

   My score: _____ Mother's score: _____ Child's score: _____

7. My children come to me for comfort and nurture. They trust me, knowing they can open up to me and be vulnerable with me.

   My score: _____ Mother's score: _____ Child's score: _____

8. My children feel safe in every way with me, emotionally, physically and spiritually. They are confident that I will fight for them in any way that they need me to. They know they have me, their father, in their corner at all times.

   My score: _____ Mother's score: _____ Child's score: _____

9. I provide for my children to the best of my ability, making them and their needs a priority.

   My score: _____ Mother's score: _____ Child's score: _____

10. I am actively and consciously engaged in teaching my children the life skills they need and in ensuring they get a good education.

    My score: _____ Mother's score: _____ Child's score: _____

11. I set clear boundaries for my children and lovingly discipline them. I am consistent in enforcing these boundaries. My children don't fear me but they respect me and what I say.

    My score: _____ *Mother's score:* _____ *Child's score:* _____

12. I lead my children by example. I make sure that the way I live is an attractive example of all I teach them and expect from them.

    My score: _____ *Mother's score:* _____ *Child's score:* _____

Don't take this as the final word on how you shape up but do use the results of this exercise as the starting point for your development as a father. Remember when you rated yourself you could only respond out of what you know of yourself. Because you have blind spots there are areas in which you may have over-rated yourself and possibly others where you have under-rated yourself. This is simply a guideline. Remember, too, that your children would be uncertain about giving you a low rating. You are their dad and they want your approval. If you have a good relationship with their mother, her rating would probably be the most accurate.

Challenge Two: Your father wound

As discussed earlier, very few men enter adulthood without some kind of wound from their father. How we deal with this wound lays the foundation for much of how we live our lives, father our children and relate to our wives.

Father wounds are passed from one generation to the next until someone has the courage and awareness to stand up and say, "Enough! It stops with me. I will break the cycle." The challenge of this book and the opportunity it offers is to be that man.

This exercise is designed to help you get in touch with any hurts that you may have received from your father. You may have had a great relationship with your father growing up, you may have had an absent father, an abusive father or not even have known your father. Whatever your history, this is a useful exercise to go through.

How would you rate your father in the 12 statements given below?

1. My dad knew my heart. He took time to really hear me, to know my likes and dislikes, my fears and dreams and what made me come alive.

   Not at all____Not really____Sometimes____Mostly____Very much____

2. My dad saw my unique talents, abilities and personality traits. He valued and acknowledged them and helped

me to discover and develop them.

Not at all____Not really____Sometimes____Mostly____Very much____

3. My dad regularly spent dedicated quality time with me.

   Not at all____Not really____Sometimes____Mostly____Very much____

4. I felt validated and affirmed by my dad.

   Not at all____Not really____Sometimes____Mostly____Very much____

5. I always knew without any doubt that my dad loved me. The words he used and the way he treated me clearly and consistently showed me.

   Not at all____Not really____Sometimes____Mostly____Very much____

6. I always knew and still know today that my dad approved of me, that he wanted and cherished me. I entered adulthood with a sense of his blessing on my life.

   Not at all____Not really____Sometimes____Mostly____Very much____

7. I could always go to my dad for comfort and nurture.

   Not at all____Not really____Sometimes____Mostly____Very much____

DAD

8. My dad always protected me emotionally, physically and spiritually. He was there for me and I knew that he would fight for me whenever I needed him to.

   Not at all____Not really____Sometimes____Mostly____Very much____

9. My dad provided for me to the best of his ability. I know that he made my needs as his child a priority.

   Not at all____Not really____Sometimes____Mostly____Very much____

10. My dad taught me to handle life well. He made sure I had the life skills I needed.

    Not at all____Not really____Sometimes____Mostly____Very much____

11. My dad lovingly disciplined me without using fear. He set clear and reasonable boundaries and was fair and consistent in making sure I kept within them.

    Not at all____Not really____Sometimes____Mostly____Very much____

12. My dad set an example for the way he expected me to live. His life matched his words.

    Not at all____Not really____Sometimes____Mostly____Very much____

MAN IN THE MIRROR

Now respond to the following five questions:

1. What are five positive life lessons that you learnt from your father?

2. What did your dad do or fail to do that hurt you emotionally or psychologically?

3. What would you have liked your father to have done differently?

4. Is there any unfinished business between you and your father? If yes, describe it.

5. Do you have any anger or resentment towards your father? If you do, write down your feelings towards him. Be honest and open; no-one has to read this but you.

Going through this exercise may have brought up some strong feelings that you will need to deal with wisely. This is a great opportunity for breakthrough in your life as a man, a son and a father. This is not about blame or revenge, it's about healing. It's not a witch hunt to find out where your dad messed up, neither is it about blaming your father for all that has gone wrong in your life. It's about setting your heart free and becoming whole. It's about taking full responsibility for your life as a man and as a father.

If you have found any residual anger with your father as you worked through this exercise, the first thing you will need to do is start the process of forgiving him. This can be very difficult but is absolutely essential for your freedom. As the well-known saying goes, bitterness is like taking poison and hoping the other person will get sick. Lack of forgiveness is toxic to our souls and lives. It is a cancer that must be removed. There is no other route to emotional wholeness. The deeper the wound, the harder it is to forgive, but the good news is that it is entirely possible.

One of the greatest aids to forgiving your father is to realise that he himself was a flawed man who carried his own father wounds into his relationship with you, his son. Your father did what he knew how to do. He fathered you out of what he had inside to call on. Don't justify or minimise the hurt that he caused you but understand where it came from.

It is very important to understand that forgiving someone does not mean you endorse the behaviour that caused pain. It is not the same as saying to someone, "What you did is okay; I have no right to be hurt." Forgiveness requires a frank acknowledgement that what someone did to you, deliberately or not, was wrong and it hurt. Only from this position of truth can you begin to forgive.

You may find yourself trying to justify your father, rationalising his behaviour and feeling guilty about condemning him. You may find yourself so filled with anger that you cannot see anything good in him. You may find yourself blaming yourself for your father's shortcomings. None of these positions is helpful. As difficult as it may be, given the emotions involved, it's important to work on being objective. See it as it is. What you feel is valid. What he did or didn't do is reality. Deal with that truth.

Forgiveness starts with a simple decision to forgive. Make up your mind to forgive your father for whatever hurt he caused you, whether by commission or omission, whether deliberate or unconscious. This is a decision to choose life and freedom and break the chains that may have been holding you back from being emotionally whole. You may not feel an instant relief; sometimes the process of letting go of the pain takes a while. Persevere. Resolve in your mind and heart that you will forgive, and the freedom will come.

The second action that you will need to take is what psychologists call re-parenting yourself. This is the process of learning all the emotional and life skills that you didn't necessarily learn growing up. It is the journey of this book and it takes most of us the rest of our lives. We men are work in progress (hopefully not just work!): growing in love, truth, awareness and wholeness.

It starts as always with awareness, with looking in your emotional mirrors and seeing yourself, warts and all, and it continues with a commitment to growth and transformation. This commitment becomes a quest and a beautiful journey of discovery and healing. There are many great resources to help you on your way. There are books, workshops, courses and men's groups to join. The important thing is that you are on the journey and that as each year goes by you are a better man than you were the year before.

Challenge Three: Self awareness

For the final exercise in this chapter you will need the input of friends and family. This beautiful exercise in self-awareness is guaranteed to touch your life. Select five people to give you feedback. If you are married, make your wife one of them. The other four can be friends, family members or work colleagues. For each one, take two sheets of paper. At the top of the first sheet write, "I respect and appreciate the following 10 things about … (insert your name)". At the top of the second sheet write, "…(Your name) would be more attractive and effective as a person if he worked on the following 10 things:"

Now ask each of the five people you have chosen to fill in the sheets. This is a powerful exercise. At the end of it you will have valuable feedback from people who know you well, which will give you deep insight into yourself and how others perceive you.

CHAPTER 9

The Man Challenge

"Men are anxious to improve their circumstances, but are unwilling to improve themselves; they therefore remain bound."
James Allen

It is one thing to know what we should be doing but it is another thing entirely to actually do it. The 12 dadverbs have hopefully given you a good idea of what it takes to be a great dad. Now it's time to put them into practice and actually be that father. Remember the parallel journey: growing as a man and at the same time becoming a great father. This chapter deals with the life skills we need to accomplish this. I have called these life skills manskills and present one manskill to work on for each dadverb.

For each manskill there is an explanation and an exercise to help you understand and develop that particular skill or quality. Once again, these exercises are just a start. They are designed to get you going, not to be the final solution to all your development needs as a man and father. Use them to kick-start your journey to authentic masculinity and great fatherhood.

DAD

Manskill One: Empathy
(Dadverb: See)

To assist you with the dadverb of seeing your child, you will need to work on the manskill of empathy. Empathy is the ability to put aside your own feelings and expectations and genuinely see and understand other people. Steven Covey tells the story of two unruly children on a train with an apparently disinterested father doing nothing to curb their bad behaviour. The other travellers in the train became increasingly annoyed by the children's disruptive behaviour until one of the passengers spoke to the father and discovered that the children's mother, his wife, had just passed away and they were in a state of shock and mourning. This gave a new perspective to the situation. Irritation turned to sympathy and understanding.

The more aware we are of the feelings, needs, desires and mental state of other people, the more effective we will be in our interpersonal interactions. The key skill is that of listening. Someone aptly said that we have two ears and one mouth and we need to use them in that proportion. We should listen twice as much as we speak. The principle is to seek first to understand before being understood.

For an exercise in developing empathy, think of three people you have been guilty of judging harshly, people whose manner or actions has roused your disapproval. For each one, write down what it is that you disapprove of. Now put yourself in their shoes; think about their background, where they come from, their circumstances. Think about why it is they do what they do and what you might do if you were in their exact circumstances with their past and the unique influences it has on their lives. If possible spend some time with them to find out more about them. Do this with an open mind and a willingness to change the way you see them and think about them.

Manskill Two: Self knowledge
(Dadverb: Identify)

To help your child discover their unique identity you need to be a man who knows who he is. Aristotle said that knowing yourself is the beginning of all wisdom. There is a powerful scene in the film *Gladiator* in which Maximus (the general who had been betrayed and sold into slavery as a Gladiator) is asked in front of a full stadium by the cowardly usurper of the Emperor's throne, Commodius, to identify himself. Not wanting to reveal his identity for fear of being executed, he replies simply, "gladiator", and walks away. The emperor is furious and demands that he reveal his true identity.

Reluctantly, knowing that this could well be the last thing he ever does, Maximus turns around, removes his mask and states with chilling conviction, "My name is Maximus Decimus Meridius, commander of the Armies of the North, General of the Felix Legions, loyal servant to the true emperor, Marcus Aurelius, father to a murdered son, husband to a murdered wife. And I will have my vengeance, in this life or the next."

Maximus knows exactly who he is, what he stands for, and what his purpose is. At the drop of a hat he can state his identity with deep conviction. Most men are not able to do this. At workshops and seminars I often ask men to contemplate this question and most struggle to come up with a convincing answer.

Our unique identity as a man is not something we easily learn in this modern world with its sterile, quick fix culture of comfort and convenience. Who are we really? What is our purpose? Is there a cause and a calling to live and die for? Most men are not sure. Before we can truly help our children to answer these questions for themselves, we need to get some answers for ourselves.

Author and theologian Frederick Beuchner said, "The place God calls you to is the place where your deep gladness and the world's deep hunger meet." Do we know what our deep gladness is? Do we know where it meets the world's deep hunger? Do we even have time to answer these questions between paying off the mortgage and keeping up with the ever present Joneses?

John Eldredge puts it beautifully when he says, "Deep in a man's heart are some fundamental questions that simply cannot be answered at the kitchen table. Who am I? What am I made of? What am I destined for? It is fear that keeps a man at home where things are neat and orderly and under his control. But the answers to his deepest questions are not to be found on television or in the refrigerator."

Every man needs to spend some time alone and in the company of other men seeking the answer to questions of identity and purpose. Mid-life crisis is born of a life lived without purpose and in search of identity. We as fathers need to help our children find theirs but first we need to find ours.

This is an exercise that cannot be rushed and is best done during some time away from your normal routine. Picture yourself in that Roman arena, surrounded by thousands of people waiting to hear the answer to the question, "who are you?" How would you answer? What would you say as you turned around, pulled off the mask of your false self and stated with deep conviction, "I am ………..." ?

The exercise is to fill in the space. Take a piece of paper and write down who you are. Spend some time over this. Pray. Ask people who know you well, use the feedback you got from the exercise in the previous chapter.

This is a profound and important question and most men live out their entire lives without really finding the answer.

Manskill Three: Time management (Dadverb: Engage)

You can tell what someone values by how they spend their time. Quite simply, if you don't spend time with your children, you don't value them. Actions do speak louder than words and sentiments are only of value if they result in action.

We live in a world of distractions and information overload. It has been said that there is more information contained in an average edition of the Washington Times than a man living in the 16th century was exposed to in his entire lifetime! Thanks to e-mail, laptops, cell phones and i-pads, work comes with us wherever we go. So does access to entertainment and the ability to communicate with anyone we know (and a whole host of people we don't), any time of day or night.

We eat in front of the television, we talk to our families while e-mailing and texting. We work hard, we play hard and we multi task hard. We are a distracted generation and it seriously impinges on our ability to connect with our children. A crucial skill to develop as a modern father is the skill of shutting out and switching off the noise and the clutter of the rest of the world and taking time to be present and in the moment with our children.

For one week take careful note of how you spend your time and then answer these questions:

1. How much time do you spend with your children over the course of an average week?

2. How much of this time is quality, uninterrupted time focusing just on them?

3. How much of this time is spent with each child alone?

4. What are the five activities that consume most of your time?

5. What are your five highest priorities in life?

6. Does the way you spend your time match your stated priorities?

7. List five things you can do to change the way you spend your time to align with your priorities. Remember that no matter what you say you value, what you actually value is what you give time to.

Manskill Four: Legitimacy
(Dadverb: Affirm)

What you need to work on here is your own sense of validity and legitimacy. In the chapter on validating, I mentioned that most men feel deep down inside that they are somehow inadequate; that the world is asking something of them that they just don't have to give. Most men posture in some way or another in an attempt to portray themselves as real men. In light of this, contemplate the following questions:

1. Do you believe that you have what it takes to be a real

man? Give reasons for your answer.

2. What qualities and strengths do you have that make you a real man?

3. What are the things that if you lost them would take away your sense of being a real man?

4. What do you believe are the qualities of a real man?

5. Ask your wife to write down what she believes the qualities of a real man are (without showing her what you wrote) and compare what you wrote to her offerings.

6. To what extent do you shape up to these qualities?

7. What can you change to align your life more closely to these qualities?

8. What do you do to make yourself feel more of a man?

9. Do you harbour any secret addictions? If you do, what is your plan to get free from these?

Manskill Five: Self love
(Dadverb: Love)

It is very difficult to truly love others when we don't have a healthy love for ourselves. Self-love is not arrogance or narcissism, it is a healthy respect and genuine care for yourself. Low self-esteem and self-hate have become silent epidemics in our age. We are bombarded with media images of what we are supposed to look like and own and the obvious conclusion is that we don't match up. Advertisers assail us with aspirational messages, all of which say "you haven't arrived yet, keep striving". In a world that values – no, worships – youth, wealth and beauty, anything less is not good enough. And even those who have everything the world applauds don't feel truly esteemed because they are valued for what they have on the outside not for who they are on the inside. All of this contributes to us feeling that we are not good enough. The natural consequence is that we find it hard to love and accept ourselves for who we are.

Consider the following questions:

1. On a scale of 1 to 10 how happy are you with yourself?

2. What needs to change for you to accept yourself more fully?

3. How successful do you consider yourself? Explain

your answer.

4. Describe the standards or benchmarks you are judging yourself against in the following areas:

   - Material success
   - Physical appearance
   - Personality
   - Socially
   - Sexually

5. How realistic are these standards? Are they fair to you?

6. From the answers to the above questions how can you assess yourself more fairly and begin to love and accept yourself more fully?

Manskill Six: Validity
(Dadverb: Bless)

Men throughout history have been passing on their blessing to the next generation by ceremony. Masculinity cannot be imparted by femininity; we men need to receive masculine blessing and impartation from our fathers. The question to ask yourself is: "Did I receive my father's blessing and masculine impartation?" Most men did not, and as a result most men struggle to do this for their children. This is a difficult thing to redeem but it is important that you do. The good news is that this blessing and impartation can come from a man or men other than your father and it's never too late to receive it.

As an exercise do one of two things, or both:

Attend a workshop with one of the many groups that work with men.

OR

Put together your own ceremony with a group of men. The key components are:

- Leaving behind the things of boyhood, cutting the apron strings.
- Being called out by other men.
- Stating your identity in front of a group of men.
- Being seen, acknowledged as a man among men, and blessed by other men.

It is quite possible to do this in your own backyard. It is even better to go away into the wild with a group of men and do it in nature. In all the times I have taken men through this process I have seen a change in the way that men walk and see themselves.

Manskill Seven: Tenderness
(Dadverb: Nurture)

Men have not often been brought up with the ability to be in touch with and freely express their feelings. Much of what has been modelled by fathers and role models has been either emotional detachment or emotional awkwardness. As a father it is crucial to learn how to know, understand and express your own emotions. This is the basis for being able to nurture our children. The scratches and bruises that our children pick up that need the most attention are not the ones they receive on their knees and elbows but those that hurt their hearts and minds. If we as fathers are not in touch with our own hearts it will be very difficult for us to understand and empathise with our children's hearts. The truth is that men can be emotionally adept. And as a father the challenge is to grow your skills in this area.

Answer the following questions honestly and objectively. It is very important that you ask your wife or girlfriend to answer them for you too, and compare what she says with your perception of yourself. If you are single ask the woman in your life that is closest to you to do so. (When it comes to emotions you can generally rely on the fairer sex to be more insightful.)

1. On a scale of 1 to 10 how in touch with your emotions would you say you are?

2. Are you comfortable in dealing with other people's emotions?

3. Are you able to express your emotions openly and honestly?

4. Describe the last time you cried as you experienced deep emotion?

5. Write down the two things that make you most angry.

6. Why do you think these two things make you so angry?

7. Write down the three things that bring you most joy.

8. Why do you think these three things bring you such joy?

Manskill Eight: Awareness
(Dadverb: Protect)

The skills needed to protect children have changed a great deal over the centuries because the world in which we live has changed so dramatically. It is no longer a simple matter of physical prowess. As a father you need to develop an awareness of the environment in which your child operates and all the potential dangers it presents. This means developing an understanding of social media, the Internet and also the social scene at the school and other places your child frequents. Children today are exposed to a lot more than we are aware of. And often they are exposed to it in our very own homes. As fathers we need to get with the programme and become aware.

So many children pull the wool over their parent's eyes about where they are going and what they are doing. And parents often don't make the effort to find out. Recently Blythe arranged to go to a concert with a group of friends. When she told me (truthfully) that all of the other parents had agreed and one father had even arranged for his driver to take them there and fetch them, I assumed that all was well. When I did some research into the nature of the concert, I was shocked to find out that it was age restricted, sponsored by a liquor company and had a line-up of unsavoury, foul-mouthed artists. I immediately called some of the other parents and became public enemy number one when the whole excursion was called off.

It's worth repeating that fathers are not in a popularity contest. We are not our children's friends. We are their guardians and gatekeepers and one of our roles is to keep them away from potentially harmful situations, even if it makes us unpopular for a time. When Blythe goes to a party or sleepover, I insist on meeting the parents, knowing what sort of parental supervision there will be. I have several of her close friends' telephone numbers in my phone in case she loses her phone or runs out of battery. If you are a vigilant, caring and involved father, your children may moan a bit but ultimately they will appreciate your heart for them. It's very important though that you show them that your concern for their safety is not because you don't trust them but because of the very real dangers they might be exposed to.

Answer the following questions. Ask your wife or girlfriend to answer them for you too, and compare her answers with yours.

1. Do you place a higher priority on being liked by your children than being their father and protector?

2. Are you involved enough to be aware of all your child's activities?

3. Do you know what websites and social media your children use?

4. Do you have any controls over what they see on the Internet and who they interact with on social media?

5. Do you give your child the clear message that the reason for your vigilance is not that you don't trust them but that you don't want them to be in any dangerous or compromising situations?

Manskill Nine: Selflessness
(Dadverb: Provide)

Keeping up with the Joneses has become a national pastime in most societies, but it doesn't lead to the optimum allocation of your financial resources. Raising children is an expensive business and it requires you as a father to prioritise the allocation of financial resources correctly. This doesn't mean giving them all they want; it means doing your best to give them all they need. It means making sure that the lifestyle choices you make are in the best interests of your children and not your own image.

If, for instance, you are offered a job in a different city with greater earnings but know that the move will disrupt your children at a crucial time of their development, what decision will you make? Will you put money and career above your children's well-being? It is always easy to rationalise the decision by saying that if you take the job you will be in a better position to provide for your children. Remember what your children need most is you.

Answer the following questions. Ask your wife or girlfriend to answer them for you too, and compare her answers with yours.

1. Do you place the needs of your children above your own when it comes to spending money?

2. Write down the 5 most important financial needs of your children

3. Are you doing enough to meet these needs? What actions will you take to make sure they are met?

4. If you are divorced or separated from the mother of your children, are you providing adequately for them? Does she agree?

Manskill Ten: Continual personal development (Dadverb: Teach)

One of the surprising things I discovered when I started running training programmes and seminars for organisations was that most people stop developing and learning when they reach a certain age. Thereafter, people seem to only change when a personal crisis leads to profound discomfort. Without being kicked out of their comfort zone by some unwelcome and unforeseen circumstance, most people stay cocooned in what I started calling tolerable mediocrity. Mediocre because they were not striving for excellence, life just happened and they went through the motions day by day. Tolerable because it was comfortable; they were not too far behind or too far ahead of their contemporaries.

DAD

I often use the example of when I was in grade eight at a school in a small town in Botswana. I could do 30 press-ups – more than anyone else in my grade. I was very content with this; smug even. Then a new kid came to town and he could do 100 press-ups. Suddenly my 30, which was the previous benchmark for me, seemed very insignificant. The bar had been raised and I was way off the mark. I learnt a valuable lesson about the danger of getting complacent and setting the benchmark too low. I began to work harder at training and soon was able to catch up with the new kid.

The stresses of life often lead us to a place of comfortable numbness. Day by day we go through the motions. That dance class you wanted to take gets put off for the 100th time, self-improvement books make way for magazines and escapist novels, your jeans slowly get tighter until one day you give in and buy the next size up. The highlight of your day becomes sinking into your sofa with a glass of wine to watch your favourite series or sitcom.

What's happened? You've become complacent. You've stopped growing. You've succumbed to the temptation to just go with the flow, to do what you need to keep your head above water and no more. To teach and equip your child for life you need to be a man who is continually growing and learning. The habit of lifelong learning and personal growth is one that makes the difference between a life of impact and significance and a life of relative mediocrity. A father who is constantly learning and growing will have plenty to teach his children about life. He will show them by example that life is more than social media and being entertained, and he will inspire them to excellence.

Answer the following questions.

1. What are you currently doing to develop yourself?

2. Write down at least two things you commit to doing to develop yourself in each of the following areas:

    - Physically
    - Spiritually
    - Emotionally
    - Mentally
    - Career
    - Relationship

Manskill Eleven: Self-discipline
(Dadverb: Discipline)

One of the greatest predictors of success in a young child is their ability to delay gratification. This was displayed in the Stanford marshmallow experiment by Walter Mischel, which tracked the success of children who participated in an experiment at the age of five. The children were seated in a room and presented with a sweet. They were told that they could have the sweet now or if they waited for 10 minutes they could have two sweets. Very few of them were able to delay their gratification and wait for the second sweet. Those who did, however, proved to be more successful in later life.

We live in a world of instant gratification with ever increasing gadgets and gizmos to make our lives more comfortable. Self-discipline is something we are called on to practise less and less. For us as fathers to discipline our children and teach them how to live disciplined lives we need to lead disciplined lives ourselves. Every area of life offers an opportunity to be disciplined or out of control.

In our words, do we lash out when angry or do we hold our tongues and make sure what we say is constructive? Emotionally, do we lose our temper at the drop of a hat or are we able to control our emotions in an appropriate way? When we eat, are we able to say no to that extra helping? When we drink, do we know when to stop or do we keep having just one more? Managing our money, are we able to resist spending or are our credit cards continually maxed out?

Complete the following exercise:

1. Rate your levels of self-discipline on a scale of 1 to 10 in the following areas of your life. Ask your wife or girlfriend to do the same and compare your scores.

    - Financial
    - Physical

- Eating
- Drinking
- Spiritual
- Emotional
- Sexual
- Time Management

2. For each of these areas write down at least one action you commit to taking in order to improve your self-discipline in that area.

- Financial
- Physical
- Eating
- Drinking
- Spiritual
- Emotional
- Sexual
- Time Management

Manskill Twelve: Integrity
(Dadverb: Model)

Integrity is simply doing what you say and living a life in which your actions match your words. Unfortunately, men whose word is their bond are more the exception than the rule today.

DAD

Children need to know that what their dad says is what their dad does. They need to see that everything their father expects of them is what their father lives and models in his own life. There is nothing that undermines who you are and what you say more than if your actions contradict your words. In a materialistic world where convenience, comfort and self-gain are often more important than people, true integrity is a rare and beautiful thing.

Our children need to see us living a life which is an attractive and desirable demonstration of all that we teach them and expect of them. If, for example, you are a religious man and would like your children to follow your beliefs, then your life needs to convince them that that is a good way to go. This does not mean regular church attendance but it does mean living a life of joy, grace and faith. If they see you grumpy and miserable a lot of the time, what does that say about the faith you are trying to teach them? If they see you attending church every Sunday but judging and criticising people all the time, you are negating the very belief system you are trying to impart to them. Your life must demonstrate your stated beliefs or else your words will be worse than meaningless, they will be seen as false.

Most men, because of a sense of inadequacy, present a false self to the world. We want to appear strong, competent, together, and manly and so we present an image to the world that is not always true. To put it bluntly, we pose. Remember the story I told of how I didn't want people to see me driving an old car? I was trying to keep up an image. Living with integrity requires taking off the masks we wear and learning to be fully who we are.

THE MAN CHALLENGE

Questions to ponder:

1. Is my life an attractive example of all I want my children to be?

2. Do I keep my word even when it hurts?

3. Are there any ways in which the person I present to the world is different to the person I am inside? In other words how do I pose, or present a false self?

4. What steps will I take to make sure that I live with a greater degree of integrity?

CHAPTER 10

The Dad Challenge

"The road to hell is paved with good intentions."
Saint Bernard of Clairvaux

Remember that no matter what you feel or what your intentions are, the only thing that counts is what you actually do. The only measure of what a man values is what he does with his time and resources. This chapter presents exercises designed to help you put into practise the 12 dadverbs.

Dadverb Exercise One: See

Without speaking to your children answer the following questions for each of them:

1. What is your child's favourite:
   - Colour?
   - Number?
   - Food?

DAD

- Song?
- Place?
- Sport?
- Pastime?

2. What makes your child's heart come alive? The thing that makes their eyes light up?

3. Describe your child's perfect day.

4. What is your child scared of?

5. Who are your child's heroes or heroines?

6. What does your child want to be when he/she grows up?

7. Now make a special time with each of your children and ask them the questions you answered above. It may take a few sessions to explore the different aspects. You don't need to tell them the answers you put down. Just use this as an exercise to get to know them. The answers to these questions will change and evolve over time as they grow up and discover themselves and their world. Keep up as they grow and change. Get in tune and stay in tune with their hearts.

8. As an on-going practice get into the habit of listening to your children. Listen both to what they are saying and what they are not saying. Observe their body language. Make it your goal to truly know what makes their hearts come alive. Look into their eyes when they talk, ask them about their day and give them your full attention as they speak. Practise reflecting back to them what you think they are saying and feeling until you get it right, until they have a deep sense that you understand and know them.

Dadverb Exercise Two: Identify

People get to know who they are by experience and exposure. Living vicariously through TV programmes and computer games will never unlock a child's true identity. You as a father need to create experiences for them, expose them to the reality of life, to history, museums, places of interest, causes, people and communities outside their own natural experience. Take them hiking, spend time in the wild, expose them to a range of things they would not normally experience. Engage in discussions with them about matters of global significance. Observe what piques their interest and help them pursue greater knowledge and experience.

DAD

Take the following actions:

1. Start a journal for each of your children in which you note your observations about each of them as a unique individual. Every time you see or hear something that gives a clue about what their unique purpose might be, jot it down and discuss it with them. This is about feeding back to them your observations and helping them to discover who they are.

2. Get into the habit of taking your children on enriching excursions.

3. Get your children involved in some kind of charitable activity to help change the world. Ask them what they would like to do to make a difference and set it up. It may be working with the poor, the elderly, the environment or animal welfare. The important thing is that they are giving and experiencing what it is to make a difference.

4. Engage your children in some after-dinner debates about world issues. Ask each of them to research an issue that interests them and to introduce the topic. Then facilitate a lively discussion around it.

Dadverb Exercise Three: Engage

The goal of these exercises is to create beautiful times of bonding with your children. This becomes harder and harder to do with each passing year. Your children will start to want to spend more time with friends and as they discover their own individual likes and dislikes they will grow more selective about how they want to spend their time. This means that the window of opportunity to regularly spend quality time with your children is relatively small. While you still can, implement the following actions:

1. Set up regular dates with each of your children where you dedicate time to be with them one on one. Ask them what they want to do and do it; just you and your child. No laptop, no cell phone calls and no texting. Ideally, this should be once a week but the minimum is once a month. If you have never done this before it may be awkward at first. You may find that you have to get to know your child in a way you have not done before. Persevere. It's absolutely worth it.

2. Start a habit of spending daily quality time with your family, without the intrusion of TV, cell phones or the Internet. The ideal time is your evening meal but each family has different schedules so work around your family timetable.

3. Try the alphabet challenge: Come up with one activity that begins with each letter of the alphabet and set a time frame to complete all 26 activities.

Dadverb Exercise Four: Affirm

For our children to take what we say to heart, it needs to be genuine. The goal of these exercises is to learn to affirm your child in a way that is both authentic and relevant.

1. Draw up a list of the qualities, personality traits, skills and abilities of each of your children.

2. Make time to comment on these to your child and affirm them verbally.

3. Get into the habit of catching your children doing something well and praise them for it.

4. Make a point every now and then of telling your children that you think they are wonderful just for being who they are.

5. Set goals with your children for all aspects of their life:

emotional, academic, sport and spiritual. Make sure you listen to what they want to do and achieve and don't impose your own expectations on them. Write down five goals for each of your children. Then discuss with each one of them and decide together on a set of goals. Make sure the goals are what they want and not what you are imposing on them.

Dadverb Exercise Five: Love

Remember the Shakespeare quote that said love not expressed is not love at all? These exercises are designed to help you express the love that you feel for your children in a way that will leave them in no doubt that they are deeply loved. Each of us has what author Gary Chapman calls a love language; a unique way in which we like to be shown love. Part of expressing love is communicating it in the way that means most to the person we are showing love to. Answer the following questions and ask your wife to do answer them for you too.

1. How do I show my children that I love them?

2. How often do I tell them that I love them?

3. How do each of my children like to be shown love?

Once you have answered this spend some time with each f your children finding out how they like to be shown love.

4. Do my actions back up my words? Do they see my love for them in my eyes, my gestures, the way that I treat them?

5. Am I consistent in showing my love? Do they see a loving dad one day and an angry dad the next?

6. What can I change in my words and behaviour to better show my children that I love them deeply?

Dadverb Exercise Six: Bless

Blessing your child happens in two ways. Firstly it is an ongoing process of approval and affirmation of your children in your daily interaction with them and secondly it is through ceremony at key milestones in their lives.

Take the following actions:

1. Develop a lexicon of words and phrases that will communicate to your children that you approve of

who they are. These are what are referred to as "being strokes"; words and actions that affirm your children for who they are, not what they do. Use words and phrases that are relevant to them and that will come naturally for you. For instance, I call Luke "My Man". This is an affirmation of his manliness. Blythe I call "My precious", or "My beautiful girl". This affirms her value to me and her feminine beauty. Think about the message you would like to communicate to each of them then write down how you would say it.

2. Get into the habit of giving your child "being strokes".

3. Use every birthday as an opportunity to celebrate your child's life, to affirm them, bless them and let them know that they are special. Some birthdays are major milestones and provide an extra opportunity to bless. When your child turns 10 (double digits), 13 (teenager), 16, 18, 20 (no longer a teenager) or 21, design a ceremony and buy a gift that has a special meaning to your child. It doesn't have to cost a lot. It just has to have meaning. You are celebrating their lives and who they are and marking the achievement of each new milestone with meaning and substance. Birthdays are not a result of something that they do but rather what they are. Celebrating achievements is important too but achievements are a result of

performance. Birthdays are a result of simply being and that's what you want to bless … who your child is.

Dadverb Exercise Seven: Nurture

It is vital that your children see you as a safe place, a person they can go to no matter what they are feeling, secure in the knowledge that you will be able to handle their tears, their vulnerability and their emotional struggles. To borrow from a sailing metaphor, they need you to be a tranquil harbour to escape from the storms of life. It is also crucial that you model men as emotionally adept, loving creatures.

If you are the kind of man who is not comfortable dealing with feelings and emotions your children may have come to see you as somewhat detached in this area. It may take some time to work through this and grow in the level of comfort you have expressing and discussing emotions. It's the classic tale of "my dad never hugged me". Become the kind of man who is equally at home sitting on the couch sharing emotions with your child as he is hiking through the forest or watching a football match with them.

The younger the child, the easier it is to show tenderness as it is mostly just physical affection and presence they need. The older they get, the more emotional intelligence it will require of you.

Respond to the following:

1. Do your children feel comfortable coming to you with their emotional struggles? Are you approachable and accessible to them? (Ask your wife what she feels about this.)

2. Can you write down five ways in which you show your children your tender side?

3. Now write down five ways you can improve your emotional accessibility to them.

4. Have a discussion with each of your children individually about their hearts. Ask them what their biggest challenge is, how they are feeling about life, school, their future, their friends; anything and everything that affects their hearts. The discussion you have will depend very much on the age and stage of your child. The objective is to get in touch with their hearts and open up the way for them to have "heart" discussions with you.

Dadverb Exercise Eight: Protect

At each stage of our children's lives the dangers they face are different and the steps we need to take to protect them differ accordingly. As toddlers we strap them up securely in a protective chair when we drive; as teenagers we WISH we could drive with them wherever they went! As a father you need to develop a clear set of standards and boundaries for your children which you communicate to them and consistently uphold.

Remember that protecting your children is as much about equipping them from the inside to be aware of and deal with life as it is about providing protection from the outside by doing whatever you can to keep them away from potentially harmful situations.

Take the following actions:

1. Write down a list of the potential dangers that your children face at their particular ages. Get the input of teachers, child care specialists and peers.

2. Engage each of your children in a conversation about the potential dangers they face. Listen at least as much as you talk. Don't make it a lecture; make it fun and informative.

3. Are you doing enough to equip your children with the awareness and skills they need to keep safe? What actions can you take to better equip them?

4. Develop a clearly defined set of principles that govern

your child's social life, the movies they are allowed to see, the places they are allowed to go to, the time they must be home, and so on. For each principle or rule have a good reason.

5. Communicate these rules to your children and be absolutely consistent in upholding them.

6. Commit to always being aware of where your children are, who they are with and what they are doing. Get the cell phone numbers of their friends and their friend's parents.

Dadverb Exercise Nine: Provide

Remember that what your children need is you (your time and involvement), a safe and comfortable home, a sense of financial security and stability, and a good education.

Respond to the following:

1. Analyse your lifestyle and honestly answer the question: "Am I optimising my time, career and lifestyle choices to best meet these four basic needs of my children?" Discuss with your wife.

2. Draw up a list of your highest financial priorities.

3. How can you be more effective in your spending habits? Write down what you can cut back on and how you can start investing wisely in things that matter instead of wasting money on things that don't really matter.

4. What is your plan for financing your children's education?

Dadverb Exercise Ten: Teach

An old Chinese proverb says: *What I hear, I forget; what I see, I remember; what I do, I understand."* Educationalists claim that we learn 10% of what we read, 20% of what we hear, 30% of what we see, 50% of what we see and hear, 70% of what we say, 90% of what we say and do. As fathers there are five keys to teaching our children the skills they need for succeeding in life.

For each of these five keys listed below, write down actions you will take to put them into practice in teaching your children.

1. Encourage them to read and discover things for themselves.

2. Verbally teach them truths about life and living.

3. Demonstrate by our own lives how to put these truths into practice.

4. Give them the opportunity to put into practice for themselves the things we have taught them by creating relevant experiences for them.

5. Coach them by showing them how to apply principles and deal with situations.

Dadverb Exercise Eleven: Discipline

Failing to discipline our children spoils them; over disciplining crushes them. We need to discipline our children with love, fairness, consistency and reasonableness. As a father you set the tone for discipline in your house but it is very important that you and your children's mother agree on these boundaries and stand together in consistently enforcing them.

Answer these questions and then get input from your children's mother.

1. Have you set clear behavioural boundaries for your children in all the important areas of their lives?

2. Have you communicated these boundaries well? Do they know where they stand when it comes to behaviour that is acceptable?

3. Are you consistent in the boundaries you set and the messages you give?

4. Are the boundaries you set reasonable, fair and age appropriate?

5. Do you eventually give in if your children ask you enough times?

6. Are there consistent and fair consequences when your children violate the boundaries you have set?

7. Do you ever punish or chastise your children in anger?

8. What is your philosophy on disciplining your children?

9. Name 10 behavioural boundaries that you have set for your children. These can be in the area of respect, table manners, words that can or cannot be used, their

treatment of the opposite sex, and so on.

10. State how you have communicated these to your children.

11. Ask your children to come up with 10 behavioural boundaries that they believe you have set for them.

Dadverb Exercise Twelve: Model

The importance of making your life an attractive example of all you want your children to be is captured in this song by Harry Chapin. Read through the lyrics and ponder the questions that follow.

Cats in the cradle

My child arrived just the other day
He came to the world in the usual way
But there were planes to catch and bills to pay
He learned to walk while I was away
And he was talkin' 'fore I knew it, and as he grew
He'd say "I'm gonna be like you dad
You know I'm gonna be like you"

DAD

And the cat's in the cradle and the silver spoon
Little boy blue and the man on the moon
When you comin' home dad?
I don't know when, but we'll get together then son
You know we'll have a good time then

My son turned ten just the other day
He said, "Thanks for the ball, Dad, come on let's play
Can you teach me to throw",
I said "Not today I got a lot to do", he said, "That's ok"
And he walked away but his smile never dimmed
And said, "I'm gonna be like him, yeah
You know I'm gonna be like him"

Well, he came home from college just the other day
So much like a man I just had to say
"Son, I'm proud of you, can you sit for a while?"
He shook his head and said with a smile
"What I'd really like, Dad, is to borrow the car keys
See you later, can I have them please?"

I've long since retired, my son's moved away
I called him up just the other day
I said, "I'd like to see you if you don't mind"
He said, "I'd love to, Dad, if I can find the time
You see my new job's a hassle and kids have the flu
But it's sure nice talking to you, Dad
It's been sure nice talking to you"

THE DAD CHALLENGE

And as I hung up the phone it occurred to me
He'd grown up just like me
My boy was just like me

After reading the words to this song (and if possible listening to it), respond to the following:

1. Name five good behaviours and habits that you are modelling for your children.

2. Name five behaviours or habits of yours that you would not like your child to develop.

3. List five actions you commit to taking to become a better model for your children.

CHAPTER 11

The Pledge

"If every man committed to just two things; being a real man and being a real dad, the world would change radically overnight."
Craig Wilkinson

The 12 dadverbs are actions that every dad can take to become a great father. My challenge to you now is to make a pledge to put these actions into practice. There is no such thing as a perfect man or a perfect father, except maybe in old TV reruns! But there are many great men and great fathers. More importantly, each of us has the capacity to become one. The pledge below is a commitment by you to your children to be and become a great father. Following through on this will change your life and theirs, and many more as a result.

By taking this pledge you are choosing to make sure that the impact you have on the lives of your children is a powerful force for good. Once you have read through it and decided that it is something you want to do, talk it through with your family and set aside an evening to say these words to them. It will be an emotional experience for you and for them. Don't do it lightly or without counting the cost. Once you say these words to them you will be accountable to them for following through with the commitment. Ask them to hold you accountable, let them know that they are free to point out to you times when they feel you are not keeping to your commitment. Let them know that although you will fail at times, you are deeply committed and willing to give your all to uphold this pledge.

The pledge is for you, your wife, your children, their children and their children's children.

The Pledge:

As a Father I realise that I am the most important and influential man in my children's lives. My life matters deeply to them and how I live my life and father them will have a lifelong impact on them. I have the power to damage them or equip them for life and the choice is mine. I realise that being a great father starts with me and how I live my life as a man. I pledge therefore to live a conscious life, to look in the mirror, to be open to feedback from those around me to the impact my actions and words have on others. I pledge to work on myself and to grow as a man and a father. I pledge to deal with any harmful habits and ways I may have and to become the kind of man I would like my son to become and my daughter one day to marry. This I pledge with the help of my God, my family and my fellow man.

I acknowledge that a real man is one who uses his strength to love, protect, care and provide for his family. A real man fulfils his responsibilities to his family, stands against any form of abuse

THE PLEDGE

and makes sure that women and children feel safe in his presence. A real man says no to any behaviour or influence which is harmful to himself or others, a real man serves his community and fights for what is right and good, a real man knows that he is a man regardless of what clothes he wears, cars he drives or house he lives in. I pledge to live my life as a real man.

As a father I pledge with all my heart and mind and strength to:

1. *Truly **see** my children, to consciously and intentionally discover the essence of who they are, what makes their hearts come alive, what excites and delights them, their hopes, dreams and fears, their likes and dislikes.*
2. ***Help** my children discover their unique identity, to be the one person they feel completely free to be themselves with, to create experiences that will help them find their passion and purpose.*
3. ***Engage** with my children, to regularly and consistently set aside quality time to be with them, play with them, enjoy them, doing the things that they love to do without distractions, to be available to them emotionally and physically.*
4. ***Affirm** my children by accepting and valuing who they are, letting them know by my words and actions that they are important, that their lives matter, and that I as their father value them deeply.*
5. ***Love** my children by the things I say to them and the way*

I behave towards them, leaving them in no doubt ever that they are deeply loved by me.

6. ***Bless*** *my children by showing them that they are wanted and that I approve of them, speaking words of blessing over them and seeking opportunities to validate them as unique and valued individuals.*

7. ***Nurture*** *my children by being tender and caring towards them, never harsh or unkind, understanding them and holding them in my embrace, giving of my strength and wisdom to comfort them when they are hurt or down or scared.*

8. ***Protect*** *my children physically, emotionally and spiritually, being aware of all that they are exposed to and the people they associate with, providing my strength, wisdom and presence to guard them from any harm.*

9. ***Provide*** *for my children to the best of my ability, putting their needs above mine to give them all that they need to live safely, comfortably and to receive a good education.*

10. ***Teach*** *my children what they need to know to succeed in life, providing them with life skills and education, and when I don't have the knowledge or skills to do so, to find someone who does to teach and mentor them.*

11. ***Discipline*** *my children by setting clear and consistent boundaries, teaching them right from wrong and not spoiling them by letting them always get what they want or crushing them by being too strict.*

THE PLEDGE

12. ***Model*** *the way for my children by making my life an attractive example of all that I want to teach them, never telling them to do what I do not do myself, always making sure that I do what I say I will.*

Signed: _____

Date: _____

CHAPTER 12

The Journey Continues

"Before I got married I had six theories about raising children; now, I have six children and no theories."
John Wilmot

Raising children well is not for the fainthearted! It will take all you can give and sometimes more and will quite possibly be the greatest challenge of your life. It's important to remember as you take on this daunting but beautiful task that we are all work in progress and need to be gracious to ourselves as we work on being a man and father. As I have written this book I have become acutely aware of the many areas in which I have fallen short as a father.

There are very few guarantees in life and your success as a father is no exception. Sometimes even when you have been the best father you know how to be your children will still play up. We cannot guarantee that our children will turn out the way we want them to, even if we do everything as right as we know how. We cannot guarantee that they will not go through a rebellious phase or make some poor choices with unpleasant consequences. Life is full of curved balls and challenging situations that we just did not plan for. What we can do is make sure that we are continually growing as men and as fathers and giving our best to be great dads.

The demands that fatherhood will make on you will change as your children grow through the various stages of their childhood. The effluence they produce as babies in nappies is very different from the kind they produce in their teenage years – and often a lot easier to deal with! A cuddly toddler is much cuter and easier to love than an angst-filled teenager, yet the importance of the father's role increases as a child grows older. The deep questions and challenges of their lives start emerging and fathers need to be there to answer. As the focus moves from physical nurture and emotional bonding to the deeper existential issues of identity and esteem, the challenge of being a father grows.

Many teenagers go through a difficult phase when they start to see some of the realities of life, how their parent's generation are messing up the environment and the economy. They become aware that leaders are often flawed and they start thinking (sometimes quite justifiably) that they could do a better job. Mark Twain once remarked, "When I was 14 I was frustrated by how little my dad knew. When I was 21 I was amazed at how much the old man had learnt in seven years".

Teenage boys experience high levels of testosterone and need to test their strength and push and explore boundaries. Teenage girls go through huge hormonal changes that often leave them feeling confused and moody. Sometimes teenagers are just otherwise. Their hormones are raging, they didn't get picked for the play or the first team; life sucks and it's mostly

THE JOURNEY CONTINUES

your fault. When this happens you need to be able to handle it with wisdom and grace. As dads we need to know that all of this is normal. The number one key is for us to be consistent.

As committed, loving, engaged fathers we need to go easy on ourselves and on our children as they pass through these normal growing pains. From toddlers to teenagers, children are not always rational, but you need to remain so at all times. Remember this is not about you; it's about your children. It's not about your heart but theirs. It's not about your ego but about doing what's best for your child.

Many fathers start getting competitive with their sons when they reach a certain age. While there's nothing wrong with a bit of healthy competition, the heart of a true father delights in his son doing better than him. One of the reasons it's so important to be secure in your own manhood is that you can put all your energy into launching your son into his own manhood, without feeling threatened or insecure in any way.

While the focus of this book has been on fathers, mothers play a crucial role as your equal partner in raising children to be whole, successful adults. A child's same gender parent is their primary role model growing up. Just as your son looks to you as a model of what it is to be a man so your daughter will look to her mother as a model of what it is to be a woman.

John Wooden profoundly observed that, "The best thing a father can do for his children is to love their mother". There is absolutely no doubt that the best environment for a child to grow up in is in a loving home with mom and dad. And if you love your child's mother with passion and loyalty you are giving your child a priceless gift. Not only are you modelling how a man should treat a woman but you are providing the glue that holds together the ideal sanctuary in which your child grows up secure and loved.

Unfortunately, two-parent homes are becoming more the exception than the norm. The sad reality is that most children do not grow up with both their parents present in the same home. However, divorce or separation does not diminish the importance of treating your child's mother with love and respect. Whatever may have happened between you and her, it is your problem and not your children's. Never get them involved. Ever.

You as their father need to model the way of love, grace and forgiveness. Treat their mom well, stick to any agreements you have with her, never speak badly of her to your kids, never let them speak badly of her. This may require you to swallow your pride and discipline your tongue but once again remember, it's not about you, it's about your children. Pull this off and not only will you live with greater peace and dignity, but you will have gifted your child in more ways than you can imagine.

Never forget that you are the man at the helm of the ship and you need to keep a steady hand and focus on the bigger picture as you navigate through the occasional storm. Keep loving, keep calm and patient, keep growing. One thing I am willing to guarantee is that if you do everything in your power to work on yourself as a man and put into practise the 12 dadverbs, you will lay the foundation for a whole and successful life for your children. How they build on it is up to them, but

THE JOURNEY CONTINUES

what they build on and the tools they have to build with are up to you.

You are the man your children need. You have what it takes. More than anything else in the world the gift of you as their father, truly fathering them, will provide your children with the launch pad they need for a life of success and fulfilment. That is our role and responsibility as their fathers. It is our duty and our privilege. Anything less is a compromise to both them and you. They deserve it and so do you.

I end with the words of William Wordsworth, *"Father! To God himself we cannot give a holier Name."*

About the Author

Craig Wilkinson grew up in three different countries - South Africa, New Zealand and Botswana. An avid hiker, mountain biker and nature lover he lives in Johannesburg, South Africa with his wife Martinique. His two adult children, Luke and Blythe, have both recently left the nest. Craig is the founder of the NPO Father A Nation (FAN), a TEDx Speaker and award winning social entrepeneur. Passionate about restoring and equipping men to be great fathers, mentors and leaders, he believes that if we can heal men we can heal the world.

Dad is available as an e-book and online course which together with Craig's book for expectant fathers called ***It's a Dad!***, can be found at **www.thedadbook.co.za.** If you enjoyed reading *Dad*, sign up for our mailing list to receive free resources and regular updates.

Made in the USA
Las Vegas, NV
28 August 2023